Food Legislative System of the UK

Stephen J. Fallows BSc, PhD
Food Policy Research Unit, School of Biomedical Sciences,
University of Bradford, West Yorkshire

Butterworths
London Boston Singapore Sydney Toronto Wellington

First published, 1988

© Butterworth & Co. (Publishers) Ltd, 1988

British Library Cataloguing in Publication Data
Fallows, Stephen J.
  Food legislative system of the UK.
  1. Great Britain. Food. Law
  I. Title
  344.104′4232

  ISBN 0–407–01540–X

Library of Congress Cataloging in Publication Data
Fallows, Stephen J.
  Food legislative system of the UK.
  Includes bibliographies and index.
  1. Food law and legislation—Great Britain. I, Title.
KD3453.F35   1988   344.41′04232   88–14488
ISBN 0–407–01540–X   344.1044232

Typeset By TecSet Ltd, Wallington, Surrey
Printed and bound in England by Page Bros. Ltd., Norwich, Norfolk

Preface

The wholesomeness, composition and safety of foods sold in the United Kingdom is a matter which has attracted the attention of legislators for many years.

The control of food standards is necessarily a complex matter and responsibilities are shared between a number of different arms of government.

The legislative arrangements (as will be shown in detail later) are shared between two major government departments, namely the Ministry of Agriculture, Fisheries and Food and the Department of Health and Social Security. On each particular issue one Department will undertake the bulk of the work: that is, it will serve as the lead Department. However, the law requires the involvement of both Departments and of the appropriate Ministers. In addition, the Secretaries of State for Wales, Scotland and Northern Ireland, together with their Departments, are also involved in the decision-making processes.

While the establishment of food laws is a central government responsibility, their enforcement is devolved to local government. Trading Standards Officers and Environmental Health Officers (among other duties) have responsibilities for:

1. Advising food producers, processors and retailers on various aspects of food law;
2. Monitoring many features relating to the quality of foods sold within their (geographic) area of responsibility;
3. Prosecution of those supplying food which in some way or other fails to meet the prescribed standards.

The many controls which apply today represent the latest derivatives of legislation dating back to at least the thirteenth century. The evolution and development of the nation's food laws over many years not only reflects the evolution of the United Kingdom food supply from basic cottage industry through to today's highly sophisticated and technically based food industry, but also illustrates the growth in sophistication of government involvement and the increased technical ability to enforce standards of purity and quality.

This book provides the reader with an introduction to the system behind the provision of food legislation as it applies today. In order to do this a number of topic areas are discussed in turn.

Part 1 sets out briefly the principles underlying the current food laws. The principal clauses of the *Food Act, 1984* are explained. Similarly, a basic summary of the more specific and detailed food regulations is given. The objective in this part of the book is to illustrate how the law currently operates; it is not intended to be a detailed legal text or even a definitive summary.

Part 2 provides the historical context for the present day-food legislation. The development of the United Kingdom's food laws is illustrated, first of all, by reference to the numerous Acts of Parliament which have been applied to foods generally. Secondly, the processes are illustrated in more detail, using a case-study approach to outline the history of the legislation applying to two common foodstuffs, bread and margarine.

Part 3 entitled 'Deciding on Legislation' sets out the processes through which change in legislation is achieved. The role of the various advisory and other bodies is particularly pertinent at this stage and the functions of advisory bodies, both national and international, are discussed.

Part 4 examines some of the major influences on the system. Two approaches are used: first, the impact of concerns about diet and health is considered as an illustration of the way that particular themes of concern may act to influence changes; and second, the role of specific interest groups is outlined to give an indication of the various groups influential in the legislative process.

The book concludes with a re-examination of the major themes which have emerged within the previous parts.

Finally, appendices provide further details about the context of the *Food Act, 1984*, notes about the main institutions of the European Community and key addresses for those who may wish to become more closely involved in the legislative processes by contributing evidence to the appropriate bodies on matters of contemporary interest.

Acknowledgements

This book presents information and ideas gathered together over a period of several years and could not have existed without the assistance of others who have been willing to share their insight and knowledge.

Particular mention must be given to the participants in a workshop held by the Food Policy Research Unit, University of Bradford in January 1985 at the Ciba Foundation with support from the Nuffield Trust. Papers prepared for this workshop by the author served as early drafts for chapters of this book. The critical comment received on that occasion, and subsequently, helped the drafts evolve into their present finished form.

In addition, a special acknowledgement must be given to my colleagues at the Food Policy Research Unit, University of Bradford without whose help and encouragement this book would not have existed.

Note on references

Each chapter is individually referenced. The following conventions have been followed:

1. The first instance of a specific and named reference to a particular Act of Parliament or Statutory Instrument in the body of the text will be referenced for each chapter; subsequent specific and named referrals will not be referenced.
2. Where documents have been used as source material but are not specifically named in the body of the text, reference will be given in all appropriate instances.

Contents

Part 1

Introduction to Current Food Law

In general, the legislation relating to food is concerned with the following: safety of food offered for sale; composition of food offered for sale, and identification of food offered for sale. These aspects have long been central to food law.

The legislation has three major functions:

1. Protection of the consumer;
2. Protection of the honest trader;
3. Promotion of freedom of choice and fair competition.

Both consumer and trader are vulnerable to the actions of the unscrupulous supplier of substandard (usually cheaper) goods. The consumer may be poisoned if dangerous ingredients are used, or cheated if poor-quality ingredients are used or if the compositional standard is below that expected by the purchaser. Similarly, the honest trader finds trading difficult if unfair practices are used by his competitors. The use of substandard ingredients can yield either greater profit or cheaper (and hence more economically attractive) goods; this is a particular problem for those foods which are difficult for the consumer to assess before purchase.

In addition to those aspects which relate specifically to foodstuffs, the sale of food is also covered by more general legislation relating to Weights and Measures and to Trade Descriptions. Although applying to food this legislation is not generally recognized as 'food law' and responsibility for administration is vested in the Department of Trade and Industry, rather than the Ministry of Agriculture, Fisheries and Food and the Department of Health and Social Security.

Food legislation in the United Kingdom is organized into a two-tier arrangement.

The general requirements, the various duties and the powers delegated to Ministers and to the enforcement authorities are set out in primary legislation by Act of Parliament. The bulk of the requirements contained within the primary legislation apply to all foods although certain sections apply only to particular foodstuffs, most notably to milk and other dairy products.

For most foods any specific rules are provided in regulations which are made under powers delegated to Ministers by the primary legislation. Similarly, regulations provide the details relating to the use of specific ingredients, labelling, contaminants and particular processing techniques.

As will be explained in more detail later, the primary legislation is subjected to the full procedures of parliamentary debate and approval. By contrast, the regulations are made by Ministers after a statutory period of consultation with interested parties. In this context, interested parties are chiefly the food trades, consumer organizations and the local authorities whose responsibility it is to enforce both the primary law and the regulations.

Primary legislation

The bulk of the primary legislation relating to foods sold in the United Kingdom is contained within three Acts of Parliament, each of which applies only within specific geographical limits.

In England and Wales, the primary statute is the *Food Act, 1984*[1]. This Act, which received Royal Assent on 26 June 1984, is based primarily on those sections of the *Food and Drugs Act, 1955* [2] which related to foods together with intervening amendments. The full title of the Act describes its function and is as follows:

> An Act to consolidate the provisions of the Food and Drugs Acts 1955 to 1982, the Sugar Act 1956, the Food and Drugs (Milk) Act 1970, section 7 (3) and (4) of the European Communities Act 1972, section 198 of the Local Government Act 1972 and Part IX of the Local Government (Miscellaneous Provisions) Act 1982 and connected provisions.

The Act came into force on 26 September 1984.

In Scotland and Northern Ireland, earlier legislation — the *Food and Drugs (Scotland) Act, 1956*[3] and the *Food and Drugs Act (Northern Ireland, 1958*[4] — remains in force. This legislation is essentially similar to that applying in England and Wales. For convenience, detailed discussion here will refer to the *Food Act, 1984*.

It should be noted that whether primary or subordinate legislation, British food laws are based on the principle that the producer and distributor of any food must be absolutely responsible for the safety and quality of such food. Any detailed provisions must be practicable and should take full account of all relevant matters, including food science and technology and the needs of the purchasing public. As with other laws intended to safeguard the public interest, the *Food Act, 1984* is part of criminal law and the offences are absolute; that is, the prosecution does not have to prove intent.

The *Food Act, 1984* is divided into seven parts covering the main points of law relating to:

I.   Food generally;
II.   Milk, dairies and cream substitutes;

III.   Markets;
IV.   Sale of food by hawkers;

together with administrative details as follows:

V.   Sugar beet and cold storage;
VI.   Administration, enforcement and legal proceedings;
VII.   General and supplemental.

Within the scope of this book it is not possible or desirable to discuss each of the sections of the *Food Act, 1984* in detail and thus emphasis will be concentrated on those topics which have required a degree of subjective decision-making in their derivation. Therefore, for the purpose of this discussion attention will be concentrated mainly on Part I, and in particular on those sections which relate to composition and labelling of foodstuffs, because these include many of the principal controls applying standards to all foodstuffs.

Part I

Part I of the *Food Act, 1984* applies to food generally and is subdivided into a number of smaller parts, each of which contains one or more sections relating to specific aspects of law (fuller details of the arrangement of all the sections in the *Food Act* are provided for reference in *Appendix 1*).

The controls outlined in Part I relate to the following major concerns:

1.   Composition and labelling of foods;
2.   Fitness of food for human consumption;
3.   Hygiene;
4.   Standards for food premises;
5.   Specific considerations relating to ice-cream, horseflesh and shellfish;
6.   Food poisoning

Each of the above concerns has attracted significant debate over the years and this has resulted in a progressive tightening of the controls. The *Food Act, 1984* (and its predecessors) primarily sets out the long-term rules and responsibilities with the day-to-day details of control being provided in subordinate regulations.

Composition and labelling of food

This part of the *Food Act, 1984* contains seven sections which form a central theme of the present legislation applying to the majority of foods.

Section 1

Section 1 refers to the preparation and sale of injurious foods and its first subsection states:

A person is guilty of an offence who

(a)   adds any substance to a food
(b)   uses any substance as an ingredient in the preparation of food
(c)   abstracts any constituent from food or
(d)   subjects food to any other process or treatment

so as (in any such case) to render the food injurious to health,
with the intent that the food shall be sold for human consumption
in that state.

The second subsection continues by stating that it is an offence to sell
such food or to offer it for sale or to advertise such food. This section
refers to four means through which a food may be rendered 'injurious
to health'. The terms used are general and are not specifically defined
in the Section or elsewhere in the *Food Act, 1984.*

As stated previously, this provision and all others contained within
the *Food Act, 1984* is one of absolute liability. There is no general
requirement to prove that an offence was committed intentionally or
even knowingly.

The term 'injurious to health' is particularly worthy of note since the
phrase is defined further in subsection 4:

In determining . . . whether an article of food is injurious to
health, regard shall be had not only to the probable effect of that
article on the health of a person consuming it, but also to the
probable cumulative effect of articles of substantially the same
composition on the health of a person consuming such articles in
ordinary quantities.

While the particular phrasing used suggests that if a food is injurious to
any one person then an offence is committed, the accepted interpretation determined by case law excludes instances where any exceptional
individual is particularly at risk. Thus, for example, if an individual is
particularly sensitive to an ingredient used this would not mean that an
offence has been committed. However, an offence would be committed
if a substantial proportion of the population were adversely affected by
a particular ingredient or process; there is no requirement to prove that
the entire population is at risk.

Section 2

Section 2 provides general protection for purchasers of food and states
that

If a person sells to the purchaser's prejudice any food which is not

(a)   of the nature, or
(b)   of the substance or
(c)   of the quality,

of the food demanded by the purchaser, he is guilty of an offence.

The key point to note from Sections 1 and 2 is the fact that there is no mention of the consumer as such; the offence is to *sell* to the purchaser, or (in Section 1), to intend that it be *sold*.

The words 'nature, substance and quality' cover all aspects of food which the purchaser has a right to expect. The words have been included in the food law since 1875 and more recently were included in the *Medicines Act, 1968*[5]. There are, in fact, three separate offences relating to the three words, although in practice it is recognized that a degree of overlap does exist.

'Not of the nature' applies principally to natural foods such as fish or fruit. For example, if coley is sold as cod, the purchaser receives something of a different variety or kind from the article asked for.

'Not of the substance' applies to aspects of composition and also includes offences relating to adulteration, foreign bodies and contamination with moulds.

'Not of the quality' refers to the commercial quality of the product in question, that is, it falls short of the quality expected by the ordinary buyer — for example, if it contains less than the expected quantity of a main ingredient or is contaminated with moulds or foreign bodies (although, as will be mentioned later when discussing Section 8, if moulds or spoilage make food unfit it may be appropriate to act under that section and not Section 2).

The phrase 'to the purchaser's prejudice' is also significant. No offence takes place if the purchaser is informed of the difference at the time of sale; neither is an offence committed if the purchaser receives an article superior to that demanded. However, case law shows that the purchaser need not be aware that the 'prejudice' exists.

Section 3

Section 3 outlines defences applicable to Section 2.

Section 4

Section 4 provides Ministers with the power to regulate the composition of particular foodstuffs as follows:

(a)   for requiring, prohibiting or regulating the addition of any specified substance or any substance of any specified class or any class of such food, or the use of any such substance as an ingredient in the preparation of such food, and generally for regulating the composition of such food;

(b)   for requiring, prohibiting or regulating the use of any process or treatment in the preparation of any food intended for sale for human consumption, or any class of such food;

(c)   for prohibiting or regulating the sale, possession for sale, offer or exposure for sale, consignment or delivery, of food which does not comply with any of the regulations . . .

(d)   for prohibiting or regulating the sale, possession for sale, or offer, exposure or advertisement for sale, of any specified substance, or of any substance of any specified class, with a view to its use in the preparation of food for human consumption, and the possession of any such substance for use in the preparation of food intended for human consumption.

The above powers are subject to certain conditions. Three main justifications are cited for establishing regulations:

1. In the interest of public health;
2. For the protection of the public;
3. When called for by any European Community obligations.

The Ministers when exercising their powers are required to

> have regard to the desirability of restricting, as far as practicable, the use of substances of no nutritional value as foods or ingredients in foods.

The powers contained in this section of the *Food Act* are wide ranging and form the principal justification for much of the subordinate legislation discussed later. Regulations made under Section 4 (or the equivalent section in the earlier legislation) relate to a range of topics. Briefly, these topics may be described as:

1. Compositional standards for named foods;
2. Controls on ingredients, especially food additives;
3. Processing controls;
4. Limitations on the maximum amounts of named substances in foods.

These points will be considered further in *Chapter 2*.

Section 5

Section 5 gives Ministers the power to require food manufacturers and importers to provide detailed particulars of the ingredients included in any foodstuff. This power is provided to enable the provisions in Section 4 (above) to be exercised. In practice, this section is very rarely exercised to find out about existing foods.

However, the provisions indicate the basis upon which controls on food additives (for example) are built. Any company developing a new substance which might be used as an additive is required to provide detailed information to justify its use, together with evidence relating to a variety of safety issues. Section 5 of the *Food Act* gives an outline of the type of information which must be provided:

(a) particulars of the composition and chemical formula of the substance
(b) particulars of the manner in which the substance is used or proposed to be used in the preparation of food
(c) particulars of any investigations carried out by or to the knowledge of the person carrying on the business in question, for the purpose of determining whether and to what extent

the substance, or any product formed when the substance is used as mentioned above, is injurious to, or in any other way affects health;

(d)   particulars of any investigations or inquiries carried out by or to the knowledge of the person carrying on the business in question for the purpose of determining the cumulative effect on the health of a person consuming the substance in ordinary quantities.

As stated above, Section 5 is rarely (if ever) used directly to order a food manufacturer to disclose information relating to specific existing foods and ingredients. Its provisions, however, do illustrate in a general manner the types of information required before a new additive (for example) is added to the lists of those substances permitted for use in foods.

Also worthy of note in Section 5 is the following statement contained within subsection 3:

No particulars provided in accordance with an order under this section, and no information relating to any individual business obtained by means of such particulars, shall, without the previous consent in writing of the person carrying on the business, be disclosed.

This principle currently applies to all information provided to Ministers in support of an application requesting (for example) that any substance be permitted for use as an additive. The wider provisions of the *Official Secrets Act, 1911*[6] set out the extent of controls relating to the disclosure of information provided to officials in the course of their duties.

For information specifically provided under Section 5 of the *Food Act, 1984*, exceptions to the above rule are set out and include the use of such information as the basis of a prosecution.

Section 6

Section 6 and Section 7 refer to the description of foods in labelling and advertising. Section 6 may be paraphrased to state that it is an offence to label or advertise a food in a manner which

(a)   falsely describes the food, or
(b)   is calculated to mislead as to its nature, or its substance or its quality.

The term 'label' is defined widely and includes tickets displayed with a food in addition to labels attached to the food or those which are printed on the wrapper or container. Similarly, advertising is also defined widely and includes all forms of food advertising including television. The formal interpretation of 'advertisement' is as follows:

. . . any notice, circular, label, wrapper, invoice, or other document, and any public announcement made orally or by any means of producing or transmitting light or sound . . . (Section 132).

Section 6 also includes particular reference to labels and advertisements which are calculated to mislead as to the nutritional or dietary value of a food; such labels and advertisements are deemed to mislead with regard to the 'quality' of the food. This subsection is currently particularly important in view of the expansion of interest in nutritional matters and the great increase in the number of food labels and advertisements which contain nutritional or dietary information.

Section 7

Section 7 provides Ministers with the power to regulate the manner in which a food is described. Regulations may include requirements relating to

(a) the labelling, marking or advertising of food intended for sale for human consumption and
(b) the description which may be applied to such food.

In practice the regulations made under Section 7 may be divided into two groups:

1. Those applying to most (if not all) foods under specific conditions. An example of this type of regulation is the *Food Labelling Regulations, 1984*[7];
2. Those which apply to specific foods or groups of foods. In general these requirements complement compositional requirements made under Section 4 of the *Food Act*. For example, the *Meat Products and Spreadable Fish Products Regulations, 1984*[8] contains both compositional and labelling requirements.

Food unfit for human consumption

The second group of sections in Part I (Foods Generally) of the *Food Act, 1984* relate to unfit foods.

Section 8

Section 8 refers to the sale of unfit food and its first subsection states:

A person who

(a) sells or offers for sale, or has in his possession for the purposes of sale or of preparation for sale, or
(b) deposits with, or consigns to, any person for the purpose of sale of or preparation for sale, any food intended for, but unfit for, human consumption is guilty of an offence.

In this context 'unfit' is taken as a matter of fact in each case. For example, a food which is mouldy is deemed unfit, whether or not it would constitute an injury to health if consumed.

The law recognizes that in practice a food is likely to be sold a number of times before sale to the ultimate purchaser and thus, for example, a retailer selling an unfit food may not be solely responsible;

the provisions therefore permit prosecution of the retailer's suppliers where appropriate.

Sections 9-12

These sections set out details relating to the enforcement of legislation relating to unfit food and to specific circumstances such as food used as prizes or in transit.

Section 13: Hygiene

Section 13 provides provisions relating to food hygiene and subsection 1 provides Ministers with the powers to:

> make such regulations as appear to them to be expedient for securing the observation of sanitary and cleanly conditions and practices in connection with
>
> (a) the sale of food for human consumption, or
> (b) the importation, preparation, transport, storage, packaging, wrapping, exposure for sale, service or delivery of food intended for sale or sold for human consumption, or otherwise for the protection of the public health in connection with those matters.

Subsection 1 (above) provides the generalities of the Ministers' powers with regard to hygiene. These powers are defined in greater detail in subsection 2 and permit regulations to be made as paraphrased below:

1. Requirements relating to food premises;
2. Requirements relating to sanitary arrangements;
3. Requirements relating to manufacture of utensils;
4. Prohibiting spitting;
5. Requirements relating to clothing;
6. Relating to animal inspection;
7. Staining of unfit meat;
8. Dealing with disposal of unfit food;
9. Prohibiting sale of shellfish from specified beds.

As with other aspects of food legislation, the detailed provisions are provided elsewhere.

Two particular points to note with regard to the system of hygiene requirements are as follows:

1. The requirements (under Section 13) do not apply to milk which is treated as a special case and dealt with separately in Part 2 of the *Food Act, 1984*;
2. Ministers are encouraged to publish codes of practice in connection with the hygiene regulations — 'for the purpose of giving advice and guidance to persons responsible for compliance with such regulations'. This point recognizes that the main function of the regulations is to *prevent* malpractices which may lead to disease rather than to prosecute offenders. This is spelt out in the key phrase 'for

the protection of the public health'. All hygiene regulations are made for this express purpose.

The remainder of Part I of the *Food Act, 1984* sets out provisions relating to:

1. The fitness of individuals to operate food premises (Section 14, for example, provides powers to disqualify caterers);
2. The registration and control of premises used for the manufacture and sale of specified foods. These relate primarily to foods which are particularly susceptible to hygiene problems, for example sausages and ice-cream;
3. Controls on the sale of horseflesh and shellfish;
4. Controls which may be applied following an outbreak of food poisoning.

Part II

Part II of the *Food Act, 1984* provides specific provisions relating to the production, processing and distribution of milk, cream and cream substitutes. In this way milk is considered as a special case by the legislative system. For virtually all other foods specific controls are given in subordinate regulations rather than in the *Food Act* itself.

Section 32

This section provides the basic definitions for terms such as 'dairy' and 'dairy farm'.

Section 33

Section 33 provides Ministers with the powers to make *Milk and Dairies Regulations*. The general subject matter of these regulations is outlined in the *Food Act, 1984* and includes the following aspects:

1.   Inspection of dairy cattle (by veterinary inspectors appointed as detailed in Section 37);
2.   Inspection of dairies;
3.   Control of facilities at dairies;
4.   Cleanliness of milk vessels;
5.   Precautions against infection and contamination;
6.   Preventing sale of infected or contaminated milk;
7.   Restrictions relating to infectious disease;
8.   Regulation of cooling, storage, conveyance and distribution of milk;
9.   Concerning labelling of milk vessels;
10. Prohibiting or restricting the addition of substances to milk or removal of milk constituents, particularly fat;
11. Setting minimum compositional standards for milk;
12. Specifying treatments for cream prior to sale;
13. Prohibiting sale of milk from cows in transit, at slaughterhouse or at a market;

14.   Setting out methods of identification of milk obtained as in (13) above.

This section also contains provisions for *Milk and Dairies Regulations* to be general or limited to a specific geographic area.

Section 34

Section 34 also relates to the *Milk and Dairies Regulations* and permits Ministers to require registration of dairymen and their premises.

Section 35

Section 35 prohibits the sale of milk from diseased cows and specifically from cows suffering the effects of tuberculosis.

Section 36

Section 36 relates to the adulteration of milk. The addition of water to milk was once a serious problem, and in order to protect the consumers' interests this practice is specifically outlawed in this section. Also prohibited is the addition of colouring matter or dried or condensed milk to milk intended for sale for human consumption.

The remainder of Part II of the *Food Act, 1984* relates to Ministers' powers to make regulations termed '*Milk (Special Designation) Regulations*' and to the various conditions and restrictions applied to these designations. The term 'special designation' refers to specific descriptions of liquid milk, namely:

1.   Untreated;
2.   Pasteurized;
3.   Ultraheat-treated;
4.   Sterilized.

Similarly, special designations are applied to cream and to reconstituted cream.

As stated previously, the use of specific legislation relating to a single food group is unusual in the primary legislation. The detailed controls relating to milk have a historical significance which derives from the following:

1.   The ease with which milk could be adulterated by dilution with water. This was not only easy for the unscrupulous dairyman to achieve but has long been recognized and objective measures of control implemented;
2.   The part which milk previously played in the spread of food-borne infections, particularly tuberculosis. Many of the specific controls which apply to the dairy industry were adopted to prevent the spread of disease;
3.   Prior to 1955 the controls relating to milk dairies and artificial cream were separate from the general food law. The previously separate *Food and Drugs (Milk, Dairies and Artificial Cream) Act,*

1950[9] was consolidated with other primary food law as Part II of the *Food and Drugs Act, 1955* which has subsequently become Part II of the *Food Act, 1984*;

In practice, many of the detailed requirements with regard to hygienic handling of milk are also applicable to other foods and to other food premises. For other foods, these controls are contained within the *Food Hygiene (General) Regulations, 1970*[10] which were made under the provisions of Section 13; this section specifically excludes milk.

Similarly, the requirements with respect to milk composition, adulteration and so on parallel the controls made for other foods under Section 4; again, this section specifically excludes milk from its application.

It is worth noting that the continuation of separate provision for milk has been questioned and the possibility of rationalization of the legislation of milk to bring it into line with that applicable to all other foods has been considered in a discussion document[11] issued by the Ministry of Agriculture, Fisheries and Food in December 1984. (This discussion document will be considered in greater detail later).

Part III

Part III of the *Food Act, 1984* sets out the general provisions of law relating to markets; similarly, Part IV sets out the law relating to hawkers. Part V relates to sugar beet and to cold storage. The sections concerned with sugar beet set out certain aspects of the government's relationships with British Sugar plc. The section concerned with cold storage is, in effect, an adjunct to the provisions in Part III by allowing a local authority to establish cold storage facilities.

Part VI

Part VI is concerned with the enforcement and administration of the various provisions contained both within the *Food Act, 1984* itself and in the numerous pieces of subordinate legislation provided in regulations.

Sections 71–75

These sections set out the administrative details defining the nature of the food and drugs authorities. For the most part, the enforcement of the provisions discussed earlier is described as the 'duty' of the local authorities.

Sections 76–86

These sections provide general descriptions of the sampling and analysis required in order to ensure compliance with the various provisions. The *Food Act, 1984* requires every food and drugs authority to appoint one or more 'public analyst' to conduct analyses of food and drugs within their area. Also specified are conditions relating to the terms of service of the public analyst. The Act also permits the authority to provide facilities for bacteriological and other examinations of samples of food and drugs.

Sections 87–91

Sections 87–91 deal specifically with enforcement and indicate the various rights of entry and seizure given to authorized officials in respect of the various provisions described earlier.

Sections 92–109

Sections 92–109 detail aspects relating to legal proceedings, appeals, compensation and arbitration.
   Of key importance are the presumptions outlined in Section 98:

(a)   any article commonly used for human consumption shall if sold, or offered, exposed or kept for sale, be presumed, until the contrary is proved, to have been sold or, as the case may be, to have been or to be intended for sale, for human consumption;

(b)   any article commonly used for human consumption which is found on premises used for the preparation, storage, or sale of that article and any article commonly used in the manufacture of products for human consumption which is found on premises used for the preparation, storage or sale of those products shall be presumed, until the contrary is proved, to be intended for sale, or for manufacturing products for sale for human consumption;

(c)   any substance capable of being used in the consumption or preparation of any article commonly used for human consumption which is found or premises on which that article is prepared shall, until the contrary is proved, be presumed to be intended for such use.

Basically, this means that if a substance commonly used in food is found to be in default of the provisions of the *Food Act, 1984* or of any subordinate regulations it is up to the defence to prove that the substance was present for a use other than for human consumption.

Part VII

Part VII of the *Food Act, 1984* includes a number of sections which provide further details and provisions which mainly permit the interpretation or enforcement of earlier sections. Three sections are particularly noteworthy in the context of this book:

Section 119

This section provides Ministers with powers to make regulations in order that British food laws accord with European Community provisions. These regulations may provide as follows:

(a) the manner of sampling any food specified in the regulations and the manner samples are dealt with, and
(b) the method to be used in analysing, testing or examining samples of any food so specified.

To date no regulations have been made specifically under these powers.

Section 131

This section provides the legislators' definition of 'food':

Unless the context otherwise requires 'food' includes drink, chewing gum and other products of a like nature and use, and articles and substances used as ingredients in the preparation of food and drink or of such products, but does not include

(a) water, live animals or birds;
(b) fodder or feedingstuffs for animals, birds or fish, or
(c) articles or substances used only as drugs.

Also contained within Section 131 is a confirmation of what is meant by a sale of a food — this is an important point as many of the principal provisions of the *Food Act, 1984* refer to offences which take place when a food is sold.

Section 132

Section 132 continues to expand the provisions of earlier sections by providing specific definitions for a large number of key words and phrases.

The main text of the Act is followed by 10 schedules which provide further details for the legislator, enforcement officers and for the legal professions.

Comment on the *Food Act, 1984*

As stated in the full title of the Act, this legislation is a consolidation of a number of earlier pieces of legislation. Its structure is in many ways based on longstanding principles which may be less valid today than was the case in the past — the whole of Part II could be cited as an example. Is there a continued need to proscribe the adulteration of milk in primary legislation while adulteration of virtually all other foods is subject to subordinate control by legislation?

The *Food Act, 1984* is the corner-stone of the system of food legislation operating in Britain today and the possibility of a new Act has been discussed widely in the mid-1980s, following the announcement of an internal review in November 1983 and the publication of a discussion document on the subject in December 1984.

Throughout the foregoing commentary on the major provisions of the *Food Act, 1984* certain features are repeatedly apparent:

1. The use for the most part of general language which requires further detail and definition;
2. The establishment of Ministerial powers to make many of the detailed provisions;
3. The detailed and general provisions are principally for the protection of the health of the public, and particularly detailed provisions are given for foods which are known to present a hazard;
4. The second feature of the provisions is their role in protecting the interests of the purchaser from unscrupulous suppliers who may otherwise operate unhygienic facilities, use substandard or dangerous ingredients or describe foods in a manner calculated to deceive.

Note on the *Food and Environment Protection Act, 1985*

As stated previously, the principal statute relating to food supply is the *Food Act, 1984*. However, other statutes also apply in certain particular circumstances. A recent example is the *Food and Environment Protection Act, 1985*[12]. This Act provides Ministers with powers to:

> authorise the making in an emergency of orders specifying activities which are to be prohibited as a precaution against the consumption of food rendered unsuitable for human consumption in consequence of an escape of substances . . . .

The above quotation taken from the Act's full title illustrates the nature of the Act's major role with respect to food supplies. It permits Ministers to take action quickly in response to incidents which lead to the escape into the environment of substances likely to contaminate the nation's food supplies. The circumstances which this Act is designed to deal with are escapes of chemical substances such as happened in Seveso, Italy or the escape of nuclear material as occurred from the Chernobyl nuclear power station in the Ukraine.

The Act applies throughout the United Kingdom (unlike the *Food Act* which applies only in England and Wales). Following an emergency a 'designated area' would be defined, within which certain prohibitions may be applied. This designated area may be:

1. Land in the United Kingdom;
2. Sea within British fishery limits;
3. A combination of land and sea.

The relevant prohibitions apply at two levels:

1. Within the designated area, specific food-related activities such as agriculture, slaughter of animals or the processing of foods may be prohibited;
2. At a national level, throughout the United Kingdom, prohibitions may be placed on the usage of items which were within the designated area after a specified time (the time of the emergency). This provision may be applied to the following:

    (a) Use of materials in the preparation or processing of food;
    (b) Landing of fish;
    (c) Slaughter of animals;
    (d) Supply of food or materials from which food may be derived;
    (e) Use of feeding stuffs.

The powers are designed to be applied quickly and controls expire after a period of 28 days unless confirmed for a longer period by Parliament.

The *Food and Environment Protection Act, 1985* also has other functions which relate to dumping of wastes at sea and to the regulation of pesticides and their usage.

During 1986 a series of orders were made under powers contained in the *Food and Environment Protection Act, 1985* to prevent human consumption of food materials which became contaminated as a consequence of the escape of radioactive materials from the nuclear reactor at Chernobyl in the Ukraine. The first order, the *Food Protection (Emergency Prohibition) Order, 1986*[13], made on 20 June 1986 designated parts of Cumbria and Wales and prohibited the movement of sheep within these areas. The supply of meat from such sheep was prohibited throughout the United Kingdom.

References

1. *Food Act, 1984*, Eliz 2 (1984 ch 30) HMSO, London. 1984
2. *Food and Drugs Act 1955* Eliz 2 (1955 ch 16) HMSO, London. 1955
3. *Food and Drugs (Scotland) Act, 1956* Eliz 2 (1956 ch 30) HMSO, Edinburgh. 1956
4. *Food and Drugs (Northern Ireland) Act, 1958* Eliz 2 (1958 ch 27 NI) HMSO, Belfast, 1958
5. *Medicines Act, 1968* Eliz 2 (1968 ch 67) HMSO, London. 1968
6. *Official Secrets Act, 1911* Geo 5 (1911 ch 28) HMSO, London. 1911
7. *Food Labelling Regulations, 1984* SI No 1305. HMSO, London. 1984
8. *Meat Product and Spreadable Fish Product Regulations, 1984* SI No 1566. HMSO, London. 1984
9. *Food and Drugs (Milk, Dairies and Artificial Cream) Act, 1950* Geo 6 (1950 ch 35) HMSO, London. 1950
10. *Food Hygiene (General) Regulations, 1970* SI No 1172. HMSO, London. 1970
11. Ministry of Agriculture, Fisheries and Food *Review of Food Legislation: Consultative Document* MAFF, London. December 1984
12. *Food and Environment Protection Act, 1985* Eliz 2 (1985 ch 48) HMSO, London. 1985
13. *Food Protection (Emergency Prohibitions) Order, 1986* SI No 1027. HMSO, London. 1986

2 Subordinate legislation

The term 'subordinate legislation' applies wherever powers to legislate are delegated by the Sovereign in Parliament (in an Act of Parliament) to a person or body. In such instances the necessity of debating each detailed provision is avoided (thereby saving Parliamentary time). A further justification for subordinate legislation is the appreciation that it is generally not possible to judge, at the time an Act is considered, precisely which detailed provisions will be required in subsequent years.

The *Food Act, 1984*[1] provides Ministers with powers to regulate foodstuffs in a variety of ways. These regulations serve to provide the detailed provisions of British food law. In this context the word 'Ministers' has a defined meaning and refers to the Minister for Agriculture, Fisheries and Food, the Secretary of State for Social Services, and the Secretary of State for Wales, acting jointly. The last two words are significant as for each issue the Ministers and their departments are required to consider everything together. In practice, for each issue one department (Ministry of Agriculture, Fisheries and Food (MAFF) or Department of Health and Social Security (DHSS)) and the appropriate Minister must take the lead. The lead Minister is responsible for dealing with any parliamentary questions relating to the subject, presenting the legislation and defending it against any critics. In general, MAFF are responsible for legislation dealing with:

1. Composition;
2. Labelling;
3. Additives;
4. Contaminants.

DHSS tends to take the lead in matters relating to

1. Processes;
2. Treatments;
3. Hygiene;
4. Toxicity;
5. Safety.

For some circumstances there will be close involvement of both MAFF and the DHSS in the preparation of regulations, while on other occasions consideration by the non-lead Ministry will be passive. However, even in such circumstances the Minister still receives all the papers and may contribute if he wishes. As a general rule the role of the Secretary of State for Wales is passive, the bulk of the work being done by DHSS or MAFF.

The system of control by subordinate legislation has evolved principally since the 1940s although some regulations have been derived from earlier controls. The system operates through the publication of regulations in the form of statutory instruments which are enforced after an appropriate period. The term 'statutory instrument' describes particular classes of subordinate legislation (including that relating to food) and was introduced by the *Statutory Instrument Act, 1946*[2] which came into force on 1 January 1948.

The *Statutory Instrument Act* sets out the mechanisms through which the Ministerial powers may be exercised; the Act replaced the *Rules Publication Act, 1893*[3].

Regulations published prior to 1 January 1948 were published as Statutory Rules and Orders. A number of pre-1948 regulations remain in force, the earliest being the *Public Health (Imported Milk) Regulations, 1926*[4].

The principal feature of the statutory instrument is the relative ease with which it may be revised or amended as needed for legislation change. (This point will be considered further in Section III). Revisions of regulations generally replace existing requirements completely whereas amendments modify particular detailed provisions. Similarly, new regulations dealing with one aspect (such as labelling) may, in turn, amend the provision contained in earlier regulations dealing with a quite separate topic: for example, the *Jam and Similar Products Regulations, 1981*[5] were amended by the *Food Labelling (Amendment) Regulations, 1982*[6]; then by the *Food (Revision of Penalties) Regulations, 1982*[7]; and subsequently by the *Sweeteners in Food Regulations, 1983*[8]; and the *Food (Revision of Penalties) Regulations, 1985*[9].

A similar pattern of amendments is found for most other food categories. For convenience, throughout this book the initial regulation only has been referenced — no attempt has been made to cite all subsequent amendments.

Food regulations

The major categories of food regulations are as follows:

Section 4   Compositional
Section 7   Labelling
Section 13   Hygiene
Section 33   Milk and Dairies
et seq

In addition, there are a number of more specific regulations which are less easily grouped.

Section 4:   Compositional

This description may be applied to a number of instances which may be grouped as follows:

Regulating composition of a food

In this instance, the regulations provide specific requirements listing the ingredients to be used. The amount of detail provided in the regulations varies with the food in question but, generally, is concerned with quantifying the proportions of major ingredients, in particular, those ingredients which characterize the product in question. For example:

1. Curry powder is required to contain not less than 85% spices, aromatic seeds and aromatic herbs (*The Food Standards (Curry Powder) Order, 1949*)[10];
2. Ice-cream is required to have a minimum fat content of 5% and a minimum of 7.5% non-fat milk solids (*Ice Cream Regulations, 1967*)[11];
3. Margarine is subject to the following limits:

    Maximum water, 16%;
    Minimum total fat, 80%;
    Maximum butterfat, 10% of fat content;
    Vitamin A, 760–940 international units per oz;
    Vitamin D, 80–100 international units per oz.

    Products (such as low-fat spreads) which do not comply with these requirements may not use the word 'margarine' in any description (*Margarine Regulations, 1967*)[12].

Specified compositional standards such as these are designed to prevent debasement of the particular food or use of a well-known name (such as butter or margarine) on a product containing key ingredients in amounts differing from that which is customary. In certain instances the compositional requirements stipulate that the food contain nutritional supplements such as vitamins and minerals. (This point will be discussed in greater detail in later chapters). A list of foods which are subject to specific compositional regulations is given as *Table 2.1*.

Prohibiting or regulating use of a substance in food

Regulations are used to state which substances may be used as additives in the manufacture of foods. Controls are applied to give lists permitting certain named substances to be used for specified purposes. For example, the *Colouring Matter in Food Regulations, 1973*[14] lists permitted colouring matter, defines the substances which may be used to dilute colours before use and specifies those classes of food which may not legally be coloured. In addition, the regulations define for a small number of colouring materials the limited range of foods for which use is allowed.

Table 2.1 Foods subject to specific compositional standards

Bread
Butter
Cheese
Cocoa and chocolate products
Coffee and coffee products
Condensed milk and dried milk
Cream
Curry powder
Fish cakes
Flour
Fruit juices
Honey
Ice cream
Jams and similar products
Margarine
Meat products
Milk and milk products
Mustard
Natural mineral waters*
Salad cream
Skimmed milk with non-milk fat
Soft drinks
Spreadable fish products
Suet
Sugar products
Tomato ketchup

* All the above requirements are made under Section 4 of the *Food Act, 1984* except those for natural mineral waters, which are made under Section 2 of the *European Communities Act, 1972*[13]

A total of eight sets of regulations (plus amendments) currently control the additives used in foods sold in Britain. These are listed below:

The Antioxidant in Food Regulations, 1978[15]
The Preservatives in Food Regulations, 1979[16]
The Mineral Hydrocarbon in Food Regulations, 1966[17]
The Solvents in Food Regulations, 1967[18]
The Colouring Matter in Food Regulations, 1973
The Emulsifier and Stabiliser in Food Regulations, 1980[19]
The Miscellaneous Additives in Food Regulations, 1980[20]
The Sweeteners in Food Regulations, 1983

In addition to controls restricting the use of food additives specifically included in the food, there are also restrictions on the maximum amounts of certain named substances which are permitted. For example, the maximum amount of lead is stated for specified foods and for food in general (*Lead in Food Regulations, 1979*[21]). Similar regulations limit the quantity of arsenic (*Arsenic in Food Regulations, 1959*[22]). The inclusion of chloroform in food is specifically banned (*Chloroform in Food Regulations, 1980*[23]) while the amount of erucic acid permitted in fats and oils is restricted (*Erucic Acid in Food Regulations, 1972*[24]).

Regulating the use of specified processes

The regulations permit restrictions on the use of specified processing techniques for the preparation of food for human consumption; similarly, in certain instances, processing is specifically required.

The *Food (Control of Irradiation) Regulations, 1972*[25] specifically prohibits the use of irradiation as a food processing technique except under very restricted circumstances — namely, for preparation of foods for patients who require a sterile diet as an essential factor in their treatment. The maximum level of irradiation permitted is stated.

The *Liquid Egg (Pasteurisation) Regulations, 1963*[26] specify that where liquid egg is to be used as a food ingredient it must be pasteurized. The conditions (temperature and length of time) are specified.

Section 7: Labelling

Labelling requirements may be either specific to a single category of food or may apply to all foods.

The requirements contained within the *Meat Products and Spreadable Fish Products Regulations, 1984*[27] provide examples of instances where particular labelling requirements apply to specified foodstuffs. By these regulations, meat products are required to be labelled with a declaration of meat (or fish) content and a statement of the quantity of added water. (There are certain exceptional meat products which are not required to provide such labelling.)

Many of the 'compositional' regulations referred to earlier contain, in addition, details specifying particular labelling requirements.

General labelling requirements are set out in the *Food Labelling Regulations, 1984*[28] which require most food labels to provide the following information:

Name of the food;
A list of ingredients;
Indication of minimum durability;
Special storage requirements;
Special conditions of use;
Name and address of manufacturer, packer or seller;
Place of origin (in certain cases);
Instructions for use.

In addition, the regulations specify further information which must be provided where claims are made relating to particular nutritional uses or dietetic properties.

Section 13: Hygiene

Hygiene regulations are primarily for the protection of public health in order to prevent the spread of food-borne disease. The regulations are generally less subjective in their derivation than those relating to composition or to labelling. There is universal agreement that food should be prepared in a clean environment and that infection should be prevented; agreement is less easily achieved when (for example) the amount of information on a food label is considered.

The current categories of food hygiene regulations are summarized in *Table 2.2*.

Table 2.2 Categories of food hygiene regulations

Docks, carriers etc
Food hygiene generally
Fresh meat exports
Imported food
Imported milk
Market stalls and delivery vehicles
Meat inspection
Meat sterilization and staining
Milk-based drinks
Poultry meat hygiene
Shellfish
Slaughterhouse hygiene

All the above are included in regulations made under Section 13 of the *Food Act, 1984*

Section 33 et seq: Milk and Dairies

Milk is regarded in law as a special food: regulations relating to compositional standards, labelling or hygiene are presented separately for milk and are made under Section 33 and subsequent sections, rather than under Sections 4, 7 or 13 as is the case for all other foods. The general principles are the same in the type or nature of the controls imposed. For example:

1. *The Milk and Dairies (Channel Islands and South Devon Milk) Regulations, 1956*[29] are primarily compositional regulations for milk of a 'specified description' — a minimum fat content of 4% rather than the 3% which applies to whole milk not of this 'specified description'.
2. *The Milk and Dairies (Milk Bottle Caps) (Colour) Regulations, 1976*[30] are basically labelling regulations which specify the cap colour code for bottled milk.
3. *The Milk and Dairies (General) Regulations, 1959*[31] and subsequent amending regulations are for the most part concerned with matters relating to hygiene and the provision of clean, uninfected milk at all stages from dairy farm production through to ultimate sale to a consumer.

Other regulations

In the context of this book it is also worth noting that subordinate legislation relating to food is not confined to regulations made under the *Food Act, 1984*. The following examples illustrate this point:

1. *The Materials and Articles in Contact with Food Regulations, 1978*[32] and subsequent amendments control the use of materials as packaging for food. The objective is to prevent the transfer of potentially

hazardous quantities of packaging constituents into the food or the deterioration in food quality due to inadequate packaging materials. These regulations are made under Section 2 of the *European Communities Act, 1972*.

2. *The International Carriage of Perishable Foodstuffs Regulations, 1985*[33] which set standards for the condition of transport facilities and state inspection particulars. These regulations are made under the *International Carriage of Foodstuffs Act, 1976*[34].

3. A number of regulations have been made under the *Food and Environment Protection Act, 1985*[35] to prohibit the movement and sale of sheep in certain areas of the country and the prohibition of their use for food. These prohibitions are emergency provisions and must be replaced after a period of 28 days, otherwise they automatically expire.

4. Standards for imported milk are controlled under the *Importation of Milk Regulations, 1983*[36] made by Ministers using powers provided by the *Importation of Milk Act, 1983*[37].

Concluding comments

The objectives behind the regulations briefly discussed here may be summed up as follows:

1. To enable purchasers of food to select foods from a position of greater knowledge than might otherwise be possible;

2. To prevent purchasers being supplied with foods which are not of specified quality and thereby to prevent specified foodstuffs from progressive debasement;

3. To ensure that foods are produced, processed and supplied to the purchaser in a hygienic and otherwise safe manner.

This brief introduction has set out to provide a general background to the types of regulations currently in force. To introduce and review each and every regulation is beyond the scope of this book and is unnecessary, as such reviews already exist for a variety of potential users. A short summary of food regulations in force is given by David Jukes in his book *Food Legislation of the UK — A Concise Guide*[38]. For those requiring greater details, direct reference to the statutory instruments and compendia of such is advised.

References

1. *Food Act, 1984* Eliz 2 (1984 ch 30) HMSO. London. 1984
2. *Statutory Instrument Act, 1946* Geo 6 (1946 ch 36) HMSO, London. 1946
3. *Rules Publication Act, 1893* Vict (1983 ch 66) HMSO, London. 1893
4. *Public Health (Imported Milk) Regulations, 1926* SR & O No 820. HMSO, London. 1926
5. *Jam and Similar Products Regulations, 1981* SI No 1063. HMSO, London. 1981

6. *Food Labelling (Amendment) Regulations, 1982* SI No 1700. HMSO, London. 1982
7. *Food (Revision of Penalties) Regulations, 1982* SI No 1727. HMSO, London. 1982
8. *Sweeteners in Food Regulations, 1983* SI No 1211. HMSO, London. 1983
9. *Food (Revision of Penalties) Regulations, 1985* SI No 67. HMSO, London. 1985
10. *Food Standards (Curry Powder) Order, 1949* SI No 1816. HMSO, London. 1949
11. *Ice Cream Regulations, 1967* SI No 1866. HMSO, London. 1967
12. *Margarine Regulations, 1967* SI No 1867. HMSO, London. 1967
13. *European Communities Act, 1972* Eliz 2 (1972 ch 68) HMSO, London. 1972
14. *Colouring Matter in Food Regulations, 1973* SI No 1340. HMSO, London. 1973
15. *Antioxidant in Food Regulations, 1978* SI No 105. HMSO, London. 1978
16. *Preservative in Food Regulations, 1979* SI No 752. HMSO, London. 1979
17. *Mineral Hydrocarbon in Food Regulations, 1966* SI No 1073. HMSO, London. 1966
18. *Solvents in Food Regulations, 1967* SI No 1582. HMSO, London. 1967
19. *Emulsifier & Stabiliser in Food Regulations, 1980* SI No 1833. HMSO, London. 1980
20. *Miscellaneous Additives in Food Regulations, 1980* SI No 1834. HMSO, London. 1980
21. *Lead in Food Regulations, 1979* SI No 1254. HMSO, London. 1979
22. *Arsenic in Food Regulations, 1959* SI No 831. HMSO, London. 1959
23. *Chloroform in Food Regulations, 1980* SI No 36. HMSO, London. 1980
24. *Erucic Acid in Food Regulations, 1972* SI No 691. HMSO, London. 1972
25. *Food (Control of Irradiation) (Amendment) Regulations, 1972* SI No 205. HMSO, London. 1972
26. *Liquid Egg (Pasteurisation) Regulations, 1963* SI No 1503. HMSO, London. 1963
27. *Meat Products and Spreadable Fish Products Regulations, 1984* SI No 1566. HMSO, London. 1984
28. *Food Labelling Regulations, 1984* SI No 1305. HMSO, London. 1984
29. *Milk and Dairies (Channel Islands and South Devon Milk) Regulations, 1956* SI No 919. HMSO, London. 1956
30. *Milk and Dairies (Milk Bottle Caps)(Colour) Regulations, 1976* SI No 2186. HMSO, London. 1976
31. *Milk and Dairies (General) Regulations, 1959* SI No 277. HMSO, London. 1959
32. *Materials and Articles in Contact with Food Regulations, 1978* SI No 1927. HMSO, London. 1978
33. *International Carriage of Perishable Foodstuffs Regulations, 1985* SI No 1071. HMSO, London. 1985
34. *International Carriage of Perishable Foodstuffs Act, 1976* Eliz 2 (1976 ch 58) HMSO, London. 1976
35. *Food and Environment Protection Act, 1985* Eliz 2 (1985 ch 48) HMSO, London. 1985
36. *Importation of Milk Regulations, 1983* SI No 1563. HMSO, London. 1983
37. *Importation of Milk Act, 1983* Eliz 2 (1983 ch 37) HMSO, London. 1983
38. Jukes, D. *Food Legislation of the UK: A Concise Guide.* Butterworths, London. 1984

Part 2

Historical Summaries

In Part I the current position with regard to the scope of food legislation, both primary and subordinate, was briefly summarized.

Examination of current legislation, however, is equivalent to examination of a photograph: it tells of the situation at a particular point in time and history. Legislation, like most other aspects of life, is not static and unchanging, but rather evolves over a period of time as new measures are added to the existing statutes or amendments made or old controls removed. The next two chapters place current legislative provisions into their historical perspective by tracing the historical antecedents of the *Food Act, 1984* and by following the development of controls which apply today to bread (a product which has a traditional role in the British diet) and margarine (a product which has been developed from advances in food technology since the latter part of the nineteenth century).

Development of primary food legislation

Measures designed to ensure that food quality is maintained have a long history stretching back over 700 years. Throughout this period the principal aim has been to protect the interests of the consumer, although it should be noted that such measures also serve to facilitate fair trade by preventing dishonest traders from competing unfairly by supplying inferior or adulterated foods.

It would appear that adulteration and/or substitution of a poorer quality item have occurred since the earliest days of the food trade.

Early history

One of the earliest examples of food legislation in Britain is an Act of 1266 which refers to bread and beer[1]. This legislation is concerned primarily with the *quantity* of food supplied rather than its quality. Objective measures of weight were available but it was not possible to make an objective measurement of quality. Quality could be assessed only subjectively or by examining the ingredients used.

Throughout the Middle Ages, scientific analysis of foods was impossible and adulteration was the norm rather than the exception. Food legislation was minimal and generally ineffective. The major group acting to maintain standards were the guilds, which could exercise a degree of influence over the activities of their members. However, this influence was chiefly confined to the towns, with the food supply for the bulk of the population in the country areas receiving little or no attention.

The extent of adulteration was substantial, with the scarcer — and hence more expensive — items particularly vulnerable. The variety of adulterants was enormous: leaves and twigs were included in ground pepper, sulphuric acid in vinegar and a wide range of grains included in supposedly wheat-only breads. Over the years, Acts of Parliament referring to specific foods sought to outlaw such practices but were generally unsuccessful. There was no general food legislation referring to all foods.

Legislation was first applied to the simplest commodities purchased on a day-to-day basis by the mass of the population. An early example was the *Assize of Bread and Ale* included in law from 1266[2]. Later, as trade flourished, legislation was applied to the scarcer imported goods of high value, an example being the *Adulteration of Tea and Coffee Act, 1724*[3].

Up to the nineteenth century, such food legislation as existed was ineffective and of an *ad hoc* nature. The nineteenth century saw significant changes which led in turn to the legislation operating today. The reasons for change were several:

1. Of primary importance was the development of scientific analysis. Until analytical techniques were developed there was no means of proving that default had taken place, neither could adulterants be identified accurately;
2. The great urban boom of the period saw a very rapid shift in the British population. There was a great movement of population away from the land and its direct, personal involvement in food production. Increasingly, the population was urban — and reliant on food retailers and the emerging food manufacturers. In the absence of effective controls the opportunities for the unscrupulous were tremendous;
3. Other social factors led to a rise in social consciousness among the influential members of society. Interest in science, together with a paternalistic desire to prevent abuses, made adulteration a matter for public debate.

In 1820 Frederick Accum published the first significant scientific document on the adulteration of foods entitled *Treatise on the Adulteration of Food and Culinary Poisons*[4]. For the first time allegations of adulteration were supported by evidence based upon chemical analyses. Parliamentary response to Accum's book was minimal and no legislation to outlaw adulteration was forthcoming. Thirty years later, in 1850, adulteration was still rife when the medical journal, the *Lancet*, established an Analytic and Sanitary Commission to investigate food adulterations. The Commissioners, Dr Arthur Hill Hassall and Dr Henry Lethaby, published their results in a series of reports printed in the *Lancet* between 1851 and 1854; Hassall later summarized these reports in a book entitled *Food and its Adulterants* published in 1855[5].

Hassall divided the adulterants into three distinct groups:

1. Fraudulent but harmless — chicory in coffee, flour in mustard, water in foods generally;
2. Indigestible but not generally toxic — sawdust, seed husks, brick dust, bone ash;
3. Highly toxic materials such as mineral pigments in the form of lead, arsenic or mercury salts, acids in products such as vinegar.

A good deal of Hassall's analysis was based on the use of the microscope which was becoming more widely available at the time. The *Lancet* reports included not only details of the methods of adulteration but also the names and addresses of the culprits. The reports stimulated a good deal of discussion in the popular Press and Parliament was forced to act. A Parliamentary Select Committee investigated the situation between 1852 and 1857. The Committee substantiated the claims published earlier in the *Lancet*. The Committee's three reports[6-8] were highly critical of the standards of food supplies and demanded that legislation be introduced to protect the public from the dangers to health presented by the adulteration of foodstuffs. The Committee set out the basis for subsequent legislation, stressing the need to utilize the emerging knowledge in analytical chemistry to detect adulteration. The Committee did, however, stress the principle that legislation should seek to prevent adulteration (including the use of education to overcome ignorance among certain sectors of the food industry) rather than act in a manner likely to interfere with the principles of fair trade. The Committee's reports, although influential, were not wholeheartedly accepted by Parliament and the resultant legislation (the *Adulteration of Food and Drink Act, 1860*[9]) was weakly drafted.

Adulteration of Food and Drink Act, 1860

The 1860 Act made the first steps towards the establishment of an effective system of food legislation and the application of controls to all foods.

The Act made it an offence *knowingly* to sell foods which contained injurious material or which was adulterated or not pure. The Act also provided county authorities with the power to establish the position of public analyst. However, there was no *duty* placed on authorities to appoint an analyst and, in fact, very few county authorities actually appointed an analyst. In addition, any public-spirited individual reporting adulteration had to pay an analysis fee which undoubtedly deterred many. Sampling was haphazard and government responsibility minimal. The ineffectiveness of the Act can be judged by the fact that, despite evidence of widespread adulteration, only one of the seven analysts appointed obtained any convictions.

A key point to note about the 1860 Act is one of principle. For the first time the principle that consumer protection measures were the general responsibility of the state was acknowledged.

Adulteration of Food and Drugs Act, 1872[10]

The law was strengthened in 1872 when all counties and boroughs were required to appoint analysts while market inspectors were given powers to enable samples of food to be acquired from suspect traders. This Act extended the provisions to include drugs and this joint Food and Drugs legislation continued until the *Medicines Act, 1968*[11] came fully into force on 1 January 1974.

The widespread appointment of public analysts led to the examination of many food samples and to many prosecutions. There were, however, weaknesses in the legislation and numerous disputes between food traders and public analysts concerning what, in practice, constituted an adulterant and what was an acceptable ingredient. In 1874 a Select Committee was established to examine the Act in detail and to make suggestions for change. The outcome of the Select Committee's report[12] was a new Act of Parliament in 1875.

Sale of Food and Drugs Act, 1875[13]

This Act is generally recognized to be the first substantial legislation, and many of the provisions set out in 1875 are still recognizable in the *Food Act, 1984*[14].

Key points to note about the 1875 Act include:

1. The Act had the express purpose of protecting the public and introduced for the first time the concept — 'to the prejudice of the purchaser';
2. The word most obnoxious to the food trade — 'adulteration' — was dropped from the title of the legislation. No doubt there had been much lobbying by the food industry of the day;
3. The law contained within the 1875 Act (and all subsequent legislation) is criminal law, not civil law, and is one of strict liability. The prosecution has no need to prove intent; earlier Acts had used the term ' . . . knowingly to . . . ' This fact alone strengthened the law considerably;
4. The Act defined 'food' very widely, as follows:

   'every article used for food, or drink, by man other than drugs or water'.

   This definition was somewhat loose and required further clarification in later legislation following subsequent court decisions;
5. The 1875 Act introduced the central provision:

   'No person shall sell to the prejudice of the purchaser anything which is not of the nature, substance or quality demanded by such purchaser'.

   This provision is essentially that currently found in Section 2 of the *Food Act, 1984*.

The 1875 Act served to eliminate much of the food adulteration then occurring, with the result that the compositional quality of food supplies improved substantially. By the turn of the century, the bulk of the nation's food supplies were free from harmful adulterants, although the simple dilution of milk with water remained a significant problem into the early part of the twentieth century. (Since milk is a food subject to a degree of natural variation, it was necessary in 1901 to set presumptive minima for the principal constituents — 3.0% for fat and 8.5% for solids not fat — in order to be able to obtain convictions for dilution (*Sale of Milk Regulations, 1901*)[15].

The late nineteenth century also saw the introduction of a number of *ad hoc* compositional measures relating to other specified foods. Those relating to bread and to butter and margarine will be discussed further in the next chapter.

The *Sale of Food and Drugs Act, 1875* was concerned only with adulteration and gross contamination; provisions relating to unsound food were provided in the *Public Health Act, 1875*[16]. However, as the science of microbiology was very much in its infancy and the mechanisms of food poisoning not understood, controls were applied only where foods showed signs of decomposition or gross contamination.

Early twentieth century

By the early part of the twentieth century the importance of a number of organisms in the causation of food poisoning was understood and a number of statutes relating to the public health aspects of food were introduced. The *Public Health (Regulations as to Food) Act, 1907*[17] provided powers to make regulations for the protection of public health.

Liquid milk is vulnerable to both adulteration and contamination. Serious attention was first given to the achievement of a clean and safe supply during the First World War, but it was not until the *Milk and Dairies (Amendment) Act, 1922*[18] that a grading system was introduced under powers given to the Minister for Health.

Regulations passed in 1925 dealt with the use of preservatives and prohibited use except in specified foods, where their use was required to be labelled[19]. Compositional regulations relating to dried milk[20] and to condensed milk[21] were also introduced in the 1920s as public health measures, reflecting their use in infant feeding. The emphasis on public health is important in this context, as the *Sale of Food and Drugs Act, 1875* did not provide any powers to regulate composition of foods in any way. Standards referred to earlier, relating to bread and margarine, were concerned with fair trade (not health) and thus required specific Act of Parliament. Such *ad hoc* arrangements continued into the twentieth century.

In 1928, the *Sale of Food and Drugs Act, 1875* was repealed by consolidation with other measures into the *Food and Drugs (Adulteration) Act, 1928*[22]. The main provisions of law remained unaltered.

The next significant step came in 1938 when the public health measures were combined with the existing food and drugs legislation in the *Food and Drugs Act, 1938*[23]. The 1938 Act strengthened the basic provisions of the food and drugs regulations by introducing disjunctive wording into the phrase 'not of the nature, substance or quality' which became 'not of the nature, or not of the substance, or not of the quality'.

The 1938 Act also introduced penalties for false or misleading labels and advertisements. This provision was especially important because there was a significant problem of false labelling. The passing off of inferior foods for some other variety had taken over from adulteration as the principal problem, and required action. The 1938 Act introduced Ministerial powers to make regulations to control both the composition and labelling of all foods.

During the Second World War the provisions contained within the 1938 Act were considered to be insufficient to deal with the special, emergency, requirements of wartime control. In 1943, an Order in Council was published which replaced and extended the provisions found in the 1938 Act. The *Defence (Sale of Food) Regulations, 1943*[24] contained provisions relating to the false labelling and advertising of food and stated that:

> A person who gives with any food sold by him, or displays with a food exposed by him for sale, a label, whether attached to or printed on the wrapper or container or not, which falsely describes that food or is otherwise calculated to mislead as to the nature, substance or quality or, in particular, as to its nutritional or dietary value, shall be guilty of an offence . . .

Identical provisions were provided with regard to food advertising. These provisions have led to the present controls in Section 6 of the *Food Act, 1984*.

The *Defence (Sale of Food) Regulations, 1943* additionally gave the Minister of Food the power to make regulations as follows:

(a)   For imposing requirements as to the labelling or marking of wrappers or containers enclosing or containing food of various kinds, and for restricting the making in advertisements of food claims or suggestions of the persence in the food of vitamins amd minerals;

(b)   For prohibiting or restricting the addition of any substance to and regulating generally the composition of, any food.

These wartime measures, established as part of much wider food controls, have formed the basis of the system of detailed control by subordinate regulations which is nowadays provided for in Sections 4 and 7 of the *Food Act, 1984*.

As a general rule, those food products which have been subject to specific compositional requirements are popular foods which are difficult for the consumer to assess before purchase, and for which a defined standard was viewed to be desirable to prevent the marketing of substandard products. The timing of introduction of control by regulation is significant on two points:

1.   The general wartime necessity for efficiency and speed provided the environment for the movement of powers from Parliament to Ministers;
2.   The wartime food shortages gave new and profitable opportunities for debasement of foodstuffs. The establishment of a wider range of standards ensured that the food and nutrition policy of the day, in which rationing was based on state-of-the-art nutritional knowledge, was not undermined by inferior food products.

Before 1943, any compositional or labelling standards had been derived on an *ad hoc* basis and had required specific Acts of Parliament (examples include the *Margarine Act, 1887*[25] and the *Artificial Cream Act, 1929*[26]).

A number of the compositional standards established under the emergency legislation remain in force today, for example standards for tomato ketchup, fish cakes and mustard.

The production, processing and sale of milk and certain milk products were further controlled by a series of enactments passed during the 1940s.

In 1954, an amending Act, the *Food and Drugs (Amendment) Act, 1954*[27] was passed and came fully into force on 1 January 1956. That date also brought into force the *Food and Drugs Act, 1955*[28]. The 1955 Act consolidated the provisions of the 1938 Act and the subsequent statutes and brought all the statute law concerning the preparation, advertising and sale of food for human consumption into a single Act. The 1955 Act continued the major provisions outlined earlier, including the use of subordinate regulations for the establishment of detailed controls relating to food composition, ingredients, labelling and processes.

In 1968, the *Food and Drugs Act, 1955* was amended significantly with the passing of the *Medicines Act, 1968* which eliminated the application to drugs. The remainder of the *Food and Drugs Act, 1955* remained in force until 1984, when the primary law relating to the preparation and sale of food in England and Wales was consolidated into the *Food Act, 1984,* described earlier. This Act merely consolidated the earlier primary legislation applicable in England and Wales (mainly based on the *Food and Drugs Act, 1955*), without introducing new material. This means that the principal provisions are over 30 years old, and may, therefore, be less effective than measures specifically drafted to deal with the food system of the 1980s and beyond.

On 23 November 1983, it was announced (by means of a written reply to a Parliamentary Question from Sir Paul Hawkins[29]) that an official review of food legislation would be carried out. On 18 December 1984, it was announced (again by means of written reply to a Parliamentary Question[30]) that the review had been completed, and that Ministers had studied the report and agreed that a consultative document discussing many aspects of the legislation be published. A few days later, the Ministry of Agriculture, Fisheries and Food made available a 99-page document[31] which discussed several areas where existing legislation was believed to be weak or presenting enforcement difficulties. The consultative document refers not only to the *Food Act, 1984* but also to equivalent legislation in Scotland and Northern Ireland. One point upon which Government sought comment was the possibility of a single new Act applicable to England, Wales and Scotland. Separate legislation would continue for Northern Ireland in view of the devolved powers of government. Any new legislation for Northern Ireland would include similar (if not identical) provisions to those applicable to England, Wales and Scotland.

The major provisions discussed in the consultative document related to the following:

1. Strengthening of the law regarding unfit food;
2. Introduction of prior approval for food premises;
3. Controls over the export of meat and other products;
4. Introduction of in-factory enforcement; this point takes note of the growth, since the *Food and Drugs Act, 1955*, in the sale of pre-

packed food and technological developments in the food industry;
5. Stricter controls over the sale of 'novel' foods and infant formulae;
6. A rationalization of the legislation applying to milk;
7. The adoption of due diligence defences where all reasonable precautions have been taken;
8. The possibility of adopting further Codes of Practice where regulations are not considered suitable.

Comments were invited from 'interested organizations representing
consumer, manufacturing, retail, health enforcement and many other
groups'. Comments were requested, not only on those points specifically referred to in the consultative document, but also on 'any matter
relevant to the Acts'. Written comments were requested by June 1985.
At the time of writing no further developments have been announced.

It should be noted that this is the second time in recent years that an
attempt has been made to make radical changes to the primary legislation. The need for replacement of the *Food and Drugs Act, 1955* was
recognized during the late 1960s but the previous review was not
followed by legislative action.

So far this discussion of the historical development of Britain's primary food legislation has traced the sequence relating specifically to
foods. It should be noted, however, that several other enactments
relate to the supply of foods and to the nature of those foods. The
Food and Environment Protection Act, 1985[32] has been referred to
earlier. A second example of major importance is the *European Communities Act, 1972*[33]. This is the principal statute relating to the United
Kingdom entry into the European Economic Community (EEC). The
Act has a significant impact on foods because it:

1. Specifically permits Ministers to introduce regulations to implement
   Community obligations — some of which relate directly to food;
2. Introduced a major change in the legislative environment, with
   European considerations gaining importance and becoming in many
   cases *the* driving force behind new developments.

Similarly, the Act, by implication, removed a degree of the UK's
potential for independent action, as new controls are required to be in
line with the principles of a multi-nation community whose declared
aim is a 'common market'; these considerations will be discussed
further in Chapter 7.

References

1. *Assisa Panis et Cerevisaiae, 1266* 51 Henry 3 Stat 1. 1266
2. Ibid
3. *Adulteration of Tea and Coffee Act, 1724* Geo I 1724
4. F. Accum *Treatise on the Adulteration of Food and Culinary Poisons* 1820
5. A. H. Hassall *Food and its Adulterants*. Longman Brown Green and
   Longman, London. 1855
6. *Report from the Select Committee on the Adulteration of Food, Drinks and
   Drugs* House of Commons, 1854–55 (432) VIII (Reprinted in *British Parlia-*

mentary Papers: Health, Food and Drugs Volume 1. Irish University Press, Shannon. 1969)

7. *2nd Report from the Select Committee on the Adulteration of Food, Drinks and Drugs* House of Commons, 1854–55 (480) I (Reprinted in *British Parliamentary Papers: Health, Food and Drugs* Volume 1. Irish University Press, Shannon. 1969)

8. *Report from the Select Committee on the Adulteration of Food, Drinks and Drugs* House of Commons, 1856 (379) VIII (Reprinted in *British Parliamentary Papers: Health, Food and Drugs* Volume II. Irish University Press, Shannon. 1969)

9. *Adulteration of Food and Drink Act, 1860* Vict (1860 ch 84) HMSO, London. 1860

10. *Adulteration of Food and Drugs Act, 1972* Vict (1872 ch 74) HMSO, London. 1972

11. *Medicines Act, 1968* Eliz 2 (1968 ch 67) HMSO, London. 1968

12. *Report from the Select Committee on the Adulteration of Food and Drugs Act, 1872* House of Commons, 1874 (262) VI (Reprinted in *British Parliamentary Papers: Health, Food and Drugs* Volume III. Irish University Press, Shannon. 1969)

13. *Sale of Food and Drugs Act, 1875* Vict (1875 ch 63) HMSO, London. 1875

14. *Food Act, 1984* Eliz 2 (1984 ch 30) HMSO, London. 1984

15. *Sale of Milk Regulations, 1901* SR & O No 657. HMSO, London. 1901

16. *Public Health Act, 1875* Vict (1875 ch 55) HMSO, London. 1875

17. *Public Health (Regulations as to Food) Act, 1907* Edward 7 (1907 ch 21) HMSO, London. 1907

18. *Milk and Dairies (Amendment) Act, 1922* Geo 5 (1922 ch 54) HMSO, London. 1922

19. *Public Health (Preservatives etc in Food) Regulations, 1925* SR & O No 775. HMSO, London. 1925

20. *Public Health (Dried Milk) Regulations, 1923* SR & O No 1323. HMSO, London. 1923

21. *Public Health (Condensed Milk) Regulations, 1923* SR & O No 509. HMSO, London. 1923

22. *Food and Drugs (Adulteration) Act, 1928* Geo 5 (1926 ch 19) HMSO, London. 1928

23. *Food and Drugs Act, 1938* Geo 6 (1938 ch 56) HMSO, London. 1938

24. *Defence (Sale of Food) Regulations, 1943* Order No 1553. HMSO, London. 1943

25. *Margarine Act, 1887* Vict (1887 ch 29) HMSO, London. 1887

26. *Artificial Cream Act, 1929* Geo 5 (1929 ch 32) HMSO, London. 1929

27. *Food and Drugs (Amendment) Act, 1954* Eliz 2 (1954 ch 67) HMSO, London. 1954

28. *Food and Drugs Act, 1955* Eliz 2 (1955 ch 16) HMSO, London. 1955

29. Michael Jopling (Minister for Agriculture, Fisheries and Food) Written Answer to Sir Paul Hawkins, Question of *Food Legislation, Hansard* 6th Series, Vol 49. Col 197. 23 November 1983

30. Michael Jopling (Minister for Agriculture, Fisheries and Food) Written Answer to Robert Jackson, Question on *Food Legislation (Review), Hansard* 6th Series, Vol 70. Col 138. 18 December 1984

31. Ministry of Agriculture, Fisheries and Food *Review of Food Legislation: Consultative Document.* MAFF, London. December 1984

32. *Food and Environmental Protection Act, 1985* Eliz 2 (1985 ch 48) HMSO, London. 1985

33. *European Communities Act, 1972* Eliz 2 (1972 ch 68) HMSO, London. 1972

4 Development of product-specific food legislation

Today, product-specific food standards legislation is organized into regulations which are subordinate to the primary food legislation contained within the *Food Act, 1984*[1]. This system is a relative newcomer when the whole history of product-specific food legislation is considered, having been developed principally following the wartime measures contained in the *Defence (Sale of Food) Regulations, 1943*[3], which gave the power to make food standards regulations to the Minister of Food. Before 1943, food standards — whether relating to specific food commodities or to food components, such as colours and other additives — were produced on an *ad hoc* basis, and legislation required the direct involvement of the Parliamentary process rather than the potentially much faster non-Parliamentary publication of a regulation by the Minister or Ministers concerned.

After the *Sale of Food and Drugs Act, 1875*[3], there was a need for equitable standards if the provisions were to be enforced. The early compositional standards were *ad hoc* and developed as the enforcement processes established *de facto* standards for a number of particular foods. In the absence of any statutory control, the individual Courts were required to establish definitions of nature, substance or quality as cases were brought by public analysts. Subsequently, the system of legally binding precedent ensured a measure of consistency from town to town. Meanwhile, the emerging food industries began to employ scientists of equivalent academic standing to public analysts, to regulate both their own products and the materials purchased as ingredients. The dairy industry were pioneers in the employment of such quality control scientists; this reflects the ease with which farmers were able to dilute milk with water.

In general, foods have specifically regulated composition only when the form of the food is such that the consumer is unable to make a reliable assessment of quality before purchase. In more recent years, the criteria have been extended and foods to which specific compositional regulations apply must be widely available and be likely to make a significant contribution to the diet.

The *ad hoc* nature of the developments in food standards reflects both the technical developments within the industry concerned and the relevant interests of groups likely to be affected by such developments.

Examination of the standards relating to specific foods provides the best method of illustrating the development of particular food standards. The contrasting case histories of margarine and bread describe some of the major developments in the formulation of regulations and the ways in which interest groups have attempted to influence the process. The studies are not exhaustive and no attempt has been made to include every minor amendment to (or call for amendment to) the legislation. Margarine is a product of relatively new technology, whereas bread is a product with a history perhaps as old as settled agriculture.

Case history 1: margarine

Margarine is a relatively new food and owes its existence to nineteenth century scientific and technical developments. It was invented in 1869 in France by Hippolyte Mège Mouries, a chemist employed by the French government. Margarine was developed scientifically as a cheap substitute for butter to counter the shortages which existed in Europe at that time[4].

The first margarine was produced by the relatively simple procedure of churning the lower-melting-point fraction of beef tallow (a cheap by-product of meat production) with skimmed milk (a cheap by-product of the dairy industry) and required relatively unsophisticated technology. The resulting product could be sold profitably at approximately half the price of butter. At the time, Britain was heavily dependent on imports for most basic foodstuffs, including butter, and as margarine became available in Europe it, too, was imported. Holland was the main source of butter sold in Britain and it was largely from Holland that margarine was imported — often supplied by companies long established in the butter industry[5]. Butter was a feature of the middle-class diet and too expensive for the mass of the urban working classes; margarine allowed the poorer part of the population a concentrated source of food energy to spread on the bread, which formed a major fraction of their diet. Britain's first margarine factory was not opened until 1889 by a Dane, Otto Monsted.

Margarine was first considered by Parliament in 1887 when a Select Committee, established to examine this foodstuff which was becoming a valuable addition to the diets of the urban poor, presented its report[6]. The enquiry was initiated from anxiety among the remaining British butter producers who were (justifiably) concerned about the ability of retailers to incorporate butter into margarine to improve its taste (and hence sales) and to adulterate butter with amounts of its cheaper competitor to their own financial gain.

Margarine was at that time popularly known as 'butterine' and it was this name which invoked greatest concern. The debate was heated, but eventually the *Margarine Act, 1887*[7] was passed. The name 'butterine' was banned and severe restrictions imposed regarding the incorporation of margarine into butter. The absolute banning of butter:margarine mixtures was not achieved and later instances of cases brought before the courts were brought because the products were thought to be 'to the prejudice of the purchaser' who was likely to be deceived. The 1887 Act also imposed restrictions on the manufacture, carriage, importation and sale of margarine. Later in 1892, there was an unsuccessful attempt (*Bill to Amend the Margarine Act, 1887*)[8] to ban the colouring of margarine, as had happened in the USA. The required standards for margarine were further tightened in the *Sale of Food and Drugs Act, 1899*[9], which limited to 10% the quantity of butter which could be incorporated into margarine and in the *Butter and Margarine Act, 1907*[10] which limited the water content of both foods to a 16% maximum. These standards continue in force, and today they are contained within the *Food Act, 1984* and the *Margarine Regulations, 1967*[11].

In general, the main theme of the legislation has acted to ensure that the quantity of fat in butter and margarine has been equal, the significant difference between the two competing foods being the sources of the fats used, the manufacturing processes used and hence the fatty acid composition of the final product.

However, since the 1940s, margarine has been fortified with vitamins A and D. Vitamin A is added at a rate equivalent to the amount in butter, while vitamin D is added at a rate approximately ten times as much as the amount in butter. This fortification was mandatory as a part of the wartime food policy which aimed to raise nutritional standards and to prevent problems associated with a restricted food supply. This fortification policy was reviewed in a report published by the *Food Standards Committee*[*] in 1954[12]. Subsequent to this report, legislation[13] was introduced which required that all margarine sold in the UK be fortified with vitamins A and D. The level of fortification is such that margarine is a significantly better source of vitamin D than its traditional competitor, butter.

The nature of the food sold as 'magarine' has changed tremendously since its invention in the nineteenth century. The colour, taste and appearance of the product have altered; concurrently, there has been a perhaps more significant change in the ingredients used in its ture. Mège Mouries used only animals fats, which he obtained by by digesting suet with an artificial gastric juice. This fat extract he then purified with acid washes and agitated with mammary tissue. The margarine was subsequently permitted to separate out and was collected. The Mège Mouries method was rapidly improved, and by as early as 1880, another cheap by-product fat source was included — cottonseed oil. Increased quantities of vegetable oils were included after the development of hydrogenation in 1903. Margarine technology *per se* (other than developments from butter manufacture) began with improvements to the emulsification process in the latter years of the nineteenth century and the development of hydrogenation in the early years of the twentieth century. Hydrogenation permitted the conversion of liquid oils into the higher-value solid fats. The major significance of hydrogenation was that it greatly extended the range of fats and oils which could be used in margarine manufacture, thereby greatly increasing the potential of the growing industry[14].

---

* The role and nature of the Food Standards Committee and other advisory committees is discussed in Chapter 6

Today, the process of margarine manufacture is extremely sophisticated: margarine can be produced from a wide variety of fat sources
and is sold as a range of products with different properties, dependent
chiefly on the content of different fatty acids. Nevertheless, it is important to note that, throughout this technological development, the legislation remains largely unchanged. The gross fat content is unaltered,
although the source, treatment and hence composition of the fat has
changed considerably. The most significant exception to this rule is
contained in the *Erucic Acid in Food Regulations, 1977*[15], which limit
the presence of erucic acid to no more than 5% of the total fat. (The
restrictions were adopted following evidence which indicated that erucic
acid can cause fatty infiltration of the heart muscles of experimental
animals.) This restriction applies to all foods containing more than 5%
fat, but was particularly enacted to limit the use of the varieties (now
largely superseded) of rape seed with high erucic acid contents in the
manufacture of foods such as margarine and blended vegetable oils.
The legislation has not acted as an impediment to the marketing of new
products.

Since the major legislation relating to margarine was last revised,
several new food products have been developed which compete with
both butter and margarine. Improved emulsifiers and the general avai-
lability of refrigerated storage today allow the inclusion of substantially
larger quantities of water than was previously possible. Similarly, products have been developed which provide the spreading characteristics
of soft margarines and the taste character of butter by mixing butter
and vegetable oils. These products are clearly outside the scope of the
existing compositional standards for margarine or for butter. It is only
by careful labelling and marketing that these products avoid the atten-
tions of the courts. 'Low-fat spreads' which contain about 60% water
would almost certainly be regarded as *de facto* adulterated margarines,
while products in which vegetable oil is combined with butterfat to give
an easy-to-spread dairy spread are *de facto* adulterated butter. This
point is a particularly noteworthy feature of the British system of food
legislation, which aims to protect the consumers' interests without hind-
ering the development of new products or unnecessarily preventing the
sale of foods of particular composition. As long as a food is clearly
labelled and does not contain ingredients which are likely to be injurious, the law permits its sale. However, the law does act to limit the
nature, substance and quality of foods known by established and legally
defined names such as margarine or butter.

The 1981 Food Standards Committee *Report on Margarine and Other
Table Spreads*[16] commented on the variety of products which were
technically feasible or marketed at that time. (Since 1981 the variety
actually marketed in the UK has increased tremendously). The Committee recommended that legislation be amended to permit specifically
— rather than to allow by default — a wide variety of products. The
Committee did suggest, however, that tighter controls be introduced
with regard to the labelling of table spreads (in particular) to ensure
that the consumer is fully appraised of the nature, substance and
quality of the products available.

To date no changes have been made to the margarine regulations
and to a large extent the Food Standard Committee's concern with

regard to fat content of margarine and table spreads has been overtaken by the wider consideration of fat content labelling of foods following the 1984 COMA *Report on Diet and Cardiovascular Disease*[17] (see page 113).

Another aspect of change in food legislation which has had a particular impact on the labelling of margarine has been the introduction in the *Food Labelling Regulations, 1984*[18] of specific controls relating to the use of claims regarding the polyunsaturated fatty acid content of foods, including detailed labelling provisions. Implied health claims with regard to polyunsaturated fatty acid content have been used commonly by manufacturers of particular brands of margarine; the 1984 regulations set out controls.

For any claim relating to polyunsaturated fatty acids in food, the following applies:

1. (a)   The food must contain at least 35% fat by weight;
    (b)   At least 45% of the fatty acids must be polyunsaturated and not more than 25% of the fatty acids may be saturated;
    (c)   The claim must be accompanied by the words 'low in saturates' or 'low in saturated fatty acids';
    (d)   The food must be marked or labelled with a declaration, expressed in grams per hundred grams or millilitres per hundred millilitres of the food, as is appropriate, stating:
          (i)   the amount of fat or oil;
          (ii)   the amount of polyunsaturated fatty acids which are *cis, cis*-methylene interrupted polyunsaturated fatty acids;
          (iii) the amount of saturated fatty acids;
          and each part of the declaration must be given equal prominence.
2.   The claim must not be accompanied by a suggestion, whether express or implied, that the food is beneficial to human health because it contains polyunsaturated fatty acids.

The above restrictions on the use of claims represents a feature increasingly present in food legislation: that is, the requirement to provide clear information about the nature of the product in question. The recommendations relating to labelling contained within the *Food Standards Committee Report on Margarine and Other Table Spreads* provide a further example. Earlier controls set out what may be referred to as 'recipe law' by defining a compositional standard for specific named categories of food — such as 'margarine'. Modern product-development practice may act to circumvent such requirements by, for example, producing a new product which has some but not all of the characteristics of the controlled product 'margarine'. The flexibility afforded by labelling requirements rather than compositional requirements suits the interests of both consumer and industry. However, there is a continued recognition of the desirability of maintaining compositional standards for key basic foods such as margarine.

Case History 2: Bread

Bread is a traditional food which has been subject to legislation for many centuries. The *Assize of Bread and Beer of 1266*[19] gave feudal courts the authority to control the weight, price and quality of bread. The basic powers of the 1266 Assize continued in force until 1709 when a new Act[20] gave local magistrates the power to specify weight, price and quality of bread after considering local market prices for grain and flour and allowing a reasonable return for the baker. Specific food standards were related to price to ensure value for money. Three categories of bread were stipulated:

1. White bread: bread made from flour from which almost all the bran had been removed;
2. Wheaten bread: bread made from flour which the coarse bran had been removed;
3. Household bread: wholemeal bread — no bran removed.

The prices were standardized by the quantity obtained for a particular price. White loaves were one-half the size of household loaves and wheaten loaves three-quarters the size. An early form of labelling was also required, stating price and weight.

In 1757 the legislation was tightened further[21] and permitted ingredients were controlled for breads of different kinds. With this Act, the compositional controls were brought into the legislation itself rather than being delegated to local magistrates, as had previously been the case. Labelling by quality became established in law, although in practice compliance was generally poor. Wheaten loaves were supposed to carry a large 'W' and household loaves a large 'H'. Acts in 1822[22] (applying to London only) and in 1836[23] abolished the Assize of Bread and extended the terms of the 1757 Act. Bread other than fancy breads and small rolls had to be sold by weight. The Acts of 1822 and 1836 remained in force until 1938 when they were repealed by the *Food and Drugs Act, 1938*[24].

During the First World War, various orders controlling the quality and composition of bread flour were made under the *Defence of the Realm* Regulations[25]. These began with the *Manufacture of Flour and Bread Order, 1917*[26] and continued into the years immediately after the War. The orders chiefly regulated the minimum extraction rates for flour (that is, the proportion of the whole wheat used to produce flour). Economic and strategic considerations limited the supply of wheat and such measures enabled a greater benefit to be achieved from a given quantity of (imported) wheat grain.

The *Food and Drugs Act, 1938* gave the Minister responsible the power to make regulations regarding composition of bread and of flour. No regulations were enacted under this Act (which required public consultation before regulations could be made) but compositional standards for flour were controlled during the Second World War by the *Defence (Sale of Foods) Regulations, 1943*[27] (which as emergency powers required no public consultation).

Wartime food regulation was stimulated by two considerations: first, there was strategic concern that maximum benefit be derived from each shipload of imported grain; secondly, there was nutritional concern for a population coping with rationing and a restricted choice of foods. In many respects the two considerations interact, as the objective was to maximize the nutritional benefit to the population. In 1940[28], and again in 1941[29], the Medical Research Council's Accessory Food Factors Committee issued memoranda which defined the desired nutritional characteristics of bread flours in the context of the then current nutritional knowledge and a recognition of the likelihood of shortage of supply.

Strategic concerns were dealt with as in the First World War by introducing a minimum extraction rate for flour in order to save grain. In September 1939, the minimum was set at 70%; by October 1939 this had been raised to 73%; in April 1941 it was raised again to 75%. These initial changes had little effect on the nature of the bread produced, but later increases in extraction rate (to 85% in April 1942 and to 90% from May to September 1948) yielded a coarser, brown, loaf. Today such a loaf might be favoured as 'high in dietary fibre' but the nutritional significance of roughage was not generally recognized in the 1940s. The controlled (National) flour continued in production after de-control of the milling and baking industries with the *Flour Order, 1953*[30] and the *Bread Order, 1953*[31] until the *Flour (Composition) Regulations, 1956*[32] which specified particular levels of nutrients rather than a minimum extraction rate.

Another grain-saving measure was introduced during the War to reduce the size of a standard large loaf from 2 pounds (lb) to 28 ounces (oz) and a standard small loaf from 1 lb to 14 oz. This measure has not been reversed, although metrication converted the larger-loaf weight to 800 g and the smaller to 400 g.

Regulation of nutritional content was the second major feature of wartime food standards and the programmes of fortification undertaken reflect a combination of available technology and contemporary nutritional opinion. At the end of the 1930s it first became possible to synthesize the vitamin thiamin (vitamin B_1) following the work of Williams and Cline[33]. In the production of white flour of low extraction rate, most of the thiamin is removed with the wheat germ and there were plans immediately before the outbreak of war to supplement white flour with the synthetic vitamin. Fortification with thiamin was promoted by government from 1940[34] at the rate of 200 mg per 280 lb sack of flour. By 1942 about 40% of flour had synthetic thiamin added. By this date the typical composition of bread was very different from the pre-war standard: ingredients which would previously have been considered adulterants were encouraged. One example of breadflour composition was cited by Calder in his book *The People's War*[35] as 82% wholemeal flour, 10% white flour, 5% barley flour and 3% oat flour. As the extraction rate approached 85% in 1942 more natural thiamin was available and the fortification ceased.

The second nutrient to be added to flour was calcium in the form of creta preparata BP (finely powdered calcium carbonate obtained from chalk). The major reason for adding calcium was the restricted supply of milk and cheese — traditional sources of this mineral. Later, as the extraction rate was raised, there were fears that the raised phytate levels in the flour (present due to the additional bran) would impair absorption of calcium from the diet, and cause problems of rickets and/or osteomalacia. Millers began to add calcium carbonate to flour from 1942 and the fortification became compulsory from 1 August 1943. In its memorandum of 1941 the Medical Research Council had advised that creta preparata be added at the rate of 14 oz per 280 lb sack of flour of 85% extraction. However, millers were initially required to fortify the flour at a rate of 7 oz per 280 lb sack. The fortification rate was later raised to 14 oz per 280 lb sack when the extraction rate was raised to 90% in May 1946.

Towards the end of the war a 'Conference on the Post-War Loaf'[36] was convened to consider future policy on fortification. The conference included representatives from government (chiefly Ministry of Food and Ministry of Health), from the milling and baking industry and from the nutritional and medical sciences. The conference considered the use of bread flours to ensure an adequate supply of four key ingredients: thiamin, riboflavin, nicotinic acid and iron. The conference concluded that flour of 80% extraction would provide sufficient thiamin, nicotinic acid and iron to ensure adequacy of supply and recommended that flour of lower extraction rate be fortified to an equivalent level. (Consideration of riboflavin was limited because other common foods are more valuable sources of this vitamin than is bread.) The conference did not review the policy of adding calcium to bread flour.

The recommendations of the Conference on the Post-War Loaf were taken up by government when the first steps to de-control were taken in 1953. The *Flour Order, 1953* required that all flour other than wholemeal be fortified with calcium and have the levels of thiamin, nicotinic acid and iron restored to those found in flour of 80% extraction.

Since 1953 the legislation relating to the fortification of flour and bread has been reconsidered from time to time. However, changes to legislation have been minimal and relate primarily to the form of iron to be used when fortifying flours (*Bread and Flour (Amendment) Regulations, 1972*[37]). The first major review[38] was undertaken by an independent panel chaired by Sir Henry Cohen in 1955 and specifically concentrated on the nutritional aspects discussed during the Conference of the Post-War Loaf. The panel's conclusions that

> the available evidence did not reveal any ascertainable difference between National flour and flour of lower extraction to which the three nutrients had been restored, which would significantly affect the health of the population in any foreseeable circumstances

but

> differences between lower extraction flour enriched with the nutrients and lower extraction flour not so enriched were significant

led to the *Flour (Composition) Regulations, 1956* which maintained the earlier fortification policy.

Changes in food technology, most notably the introduction in the early 1960s of the Chorleywood bread-making process (CBP)[39], led to amendment of the list of permitted ingredients beginning with the *Bread and Flour Regulations, 1963*[40]. Until the *Bread and Flour Regulations, 1984*[41] the use of several additives in the manufacture of wholemeal bread was not permitted and the traditional production methods had to be used for this particular variety.

The use of various additives in food manufacture has been a subject for official debate for many years. The debate with respect to bread and flour has been particularly important in view of the significant contribution made by bread to the typical British diet. The discussions from the 1920s to 1950s were summarized by the Food Standards Committee (see Chapter 6) in its 1960 *Report·on Bread and Flour*[42].

The use of improvers in wholemeal flours was first recommended in a second report on Bread and Flour[43] from the Food Standards Committee and the Food Additives and Contaminants Committee which was published in 1974. There were strong arguments for and against. Traditional wholemeal bread (without improvers) was said by many people to keep less well than white bread; bakers claimed that this was because they were unable to use the optimal mix of ingredients, i.e. they were not allowed to use improvers. Furthermore, without using improvers, bakers were unable to use much of their available machinery (Chorleywood Process) for the production of wholemeal bread and this may have acted to limit supplies and hence consumption. However, 'wholemeal' has connotations of 'natural' and there are many people who feel that wholemeal bread ought to be produced using the minimum number of additives and processing aids. The conclusions of the Food Standards Committee/Food Additives and Contaminants Committee with respect to flour improvers were repeated in 1981 in a report from the Committee on Medical Aspects of Food Policy (COMA)[44].

The debate over the use of improvers in wholemeal flour is a complex mixture of subjective opinion and scientific/technical fact. The balance of opinion within the official bodies which reviewed the topic is that the production of wholemeal bread, which is attractive to a wider sector of the community, provides greater benefit than does the preservation of an ill-defined aura of 'natural'.

The rules relating to the use of improvers were changed in the *Bread and Flour Regulations, 1984* and since that date all breads may contain improvers which must be declared in the case of both pre-packed and non-prepacked breads.

The 1984 regulations, in addition, specified conditions relating to the name of the bread by defining, for example, wholemeal, brown, wheatgerm and white breads and banning the use of the term 'wheatmeal'. The regulations came fully into force on 1 July 1986 after a two-year transition period.

A point worth noting here is the fact that wholemeal breads have become significantly more popular in the years since 1984; the extent to which changes in the permitted ingredients have contributed to this change must remain a matter of speculation.

A second major issue raised by the 1981 COMA report on bread and flour related to the policy of fortification begun in the 1940s. The committee reviewed prevailing nutritional opinion and recommended that the addition of calcium carbonate and the restoration of iron, thiamin and nicotinic acid should no longer be mandatory for any type of bread. This recommendation was criticized by many[45] who feared that it might put some groups in the population at risk of nutritional deficiency. Geriatricians, in particular, expressed concern over potential thiamin deficiency among the elderly[46].

The early proposals for revisions to legislation, issued in 1983, followed the COMA panel's advice. However, the extent of public pressure on those responsible for drafting and administering the food standards legislation proved sufficient on this issue to force a change of strategy and further proposals in March 1984 reinstated the requirement to fortify as in previous regulations.

The current position with regard to nutritional supplementation is contained in the *Bread and Flour Regulations, 1984* and is as follows:

1. Calcium carbonate: not less than 235 milligrams and not more than 390 milligrams per hundred grams of flour. Purity and granular size standards are given;
2. Iron: not less than 1.65 milligrams per hundred grams of flour. Iron may be provided in one of a number of forms. Purity standards are defined for each;
3. Thiamin: not less than 0.24 milligrams per hundred grams of flour. Purity standards are defined;
4. Nicotinic acid or nicotinamide: not less than 1.65 milligrams per 100 grams of flour. Purity standards are defined.

These requirements are identical to those in force since the *Flour (Composition) Regulations, 1956*.

The recent history of the control of bread composition provides a useful case history of the way in which the composition and/or labelling of a food or group of foods may be reviewed by one or more advisory committees over a period of time. It also illustrates the way in which proposals for changes to legislation may be influenced by a well-organized lobby. The way in which legislation proceeds from initial concept through to the statute book is considered in greater detail in the next section.

References

1. *Food Act, 1984* Eliz 2 (1984 ch 30). HMSO, London. 1984
2. *Defence (Sale of Food) Regulations, 1943* Order No 1553. HMSO, London. 1943
3. *Sale of Food and Drugs Act, 1875* Vict (1875 ch 63). HMSO, London. 1875
4. Clayton, W. *Margarine*. Longmans, Green and Co, London. 1920
5. Wilson C. *The History of Unilever: A Study in Economic Growth and Social Change, Volume II*. Cassell and Co, London. 1954
6. *Report of Select Committee: Butter Substitutes Bill*, HMSO, London. 1882
7. *Margarine Act, 1887* Vict (1887 ch 29). HMSO, London. 1887
8. *Bill to Amend the Margarine Act, 1887*. House of Commons, London. 1883
9. *Sale of Food and Drugs Act, 1899* Vict (1899 ch 51). HMSO, London. 1899

10. *Butter and Margarine Act, 1907* Edw 7 (1907 ch 21). HMSO, London. 1907
     1907
11. *Margarine Regulations, 1967* SI No 1867. HMSO, London. 1967
12. Ministry of Agriculture, Fisheries and Food *Food Standards Committee
     Report on Vitaminisation of Margarine* FSC/REP/36. HMSO, London. 1954
13. *Food Standards (Margarine Order), 1954* SI No 613. HMSO, London. 1954
14. van Stuyvenberg, J. H. *Margarine: An Economic, Social and Scientific
     History, 1929–1969.* Liverpool University Press, Liverpool. 1969
15. *Erucic Acid in Food Regulations, 1977* SI No 691. HMSO, London. 1977
16. Ministry of Agriculture, Fisheries and Food *Food Standards Committee
     Report on Margarine and Other Table Spreads.* FSC/REP/74. HMSO,
     London. 1981
17. Department of Health and Social Security *Diet and Cardiovascular Disease.
     Report of the Panel on Diet in Relation to Cardiovascular Disease.
     Committee on Medical Aspects of Food Policy. Report on Health and Social
     Subjects No 28.* HMSO, London. 1984
18. *Food Labelling Regulations, 1984* SI No 1305. HMSO, London. 1984
19. *Assisa Panis et Cerevisiae, 1266* 51 Henry III Stat 1. 1266
20. *Bread Act, 1709* Anne (1709 ch 19). Parliament, London. 1709
21. *Bread Act, 1757* Geo II (1757 ch 29). Parliament, London. 1757
22. *Bread Act, 1822* Geo 4 (1822 ch 107). HMSO, London. 1822
23. *Bread Act, 1836* Will 2 (1836 ch 37). HMSO, London. 1836
24. *Food and Drugs Act, 1938* Geo 6 (1938 ch 56). HMSO, London. 1938
25. *Defence of the Realm (Consolidation) Act* Geo 5 (1914 ch 8). HMSO,
     London. 1914
26. *Manufacture of Flour and Bread Order, 1917* SR & O No 62. HMSO,
     London. 1917
27. *Defence (Sale of Food) Regulations, 1943* Order No 1553. HMSO, London.
     1943
28. Medical Research Council Accessory Food Factors Committee. MRC
     Memorandum on Bread. *Lancet* **ii**, 143. 1940
29. Medical Research Council Accessory Food Factors Committee. National
     Flour: A Second Memorandum. *Lancet* **i**, 702–704. 1941
30. *Flour Order, 1953* SI No 1281. HMSO, London. 1953
31. *Bread Order, 1953* SI No 1283. HMSO, London. 1953
32. *Flour (Composition) Regulations, 1956* SI No 1183. HMSO, London. 1953
33. Williams, R. R. and Cline, J. K. Synthesis of Vitamin B_1. *Journal of the
     American Chemical Society* **58**, (8), 1504–1505. 1936
34. Elton, G. A. *The Fortification of Flour.* In: A Spicer (Ed), *Bread: Social,
     Nutritional and Agricultural Aspects of Wheaten Bread.* Applied Science
     Publishers, Barking. 1975
35. Calder, A. *The People's War: Britain 1939–45.* Jonathan Cape, London.
     1969
36. Ministry of Food. *Report of the Conference on the Post-War Loaf* Cmd
     6701. HMSO, London. 1945
37. *Bread and Flour (Amendment) Regulations, 1972* SI No 1391. HMSO,
     London. 1972
38. Ministry of Agriculture, Fisheries and Food. *Report of the Panel on
     Composition and Nutritive Value of Flour.* HMSO, London. 1956
39. Chamberlain, N., Collins, T. H. and Elton, G. A. H. The Chorleywood
     Bread Process. *Bakers Digest* **36**, (5), 52. 1962
40. *Bread and Flour Regulations, 1963* SI No 1435. HMSO, London. 1963
41. *Bread and Flour Regulations, 1984* SI No 1304. HMSO, London. 1984
42. Ministry of Agriculture, Fisheries and Food. *Food Standards Committee
     Report on Bread and Flour* FSC/REP/43. HMSO, London. 1960
43. Ministry of Agriculture, Fisheries and Food. *Food Standards Committee
     Second Report on Bread and Flour* FSC/REP/61. HMSO, London. 1974
44. Department of Health and Social Security *Nutritional Aspects of Bread and*

Flour. Report of the Panel on Bread Flour and other Cereal Products, Committee on Medical Aspects of Food Policy. Report on Health and Social Subjects No 23. HMSO, London. 1981

45. See, for example, articles and correspondence published in the *Sunday Times*, 10 July, 17 July and 24 July 1983; also *The Grocer*, 10 December 1983

46. Information Department, Age Concern. *An Aspect of the Proposals for New Bread and Flour Regulations* Age Concern England, Mitcham. 1983

Part 3

Deciding on Legislation

Initiating change

All legislation is subject to periodic amendment or replacement as changes take place within society as a whole. Legislation relating to food (whether primary or subordinate) is no exception. In general, most changes to food legislation are relatively minor amendments to either the *Food Act* or to specific regulations. Some amendments arise directly from legislation relating specifically to food whereas others are more indirect, resulting from changes to legislation applying to quite separate topics.

From time to time, existing legislation will be replaced completely by either a new Act or new regulations. Such replacements are relatively rare and are initiated only after careful consideration of the issues involved. This is particularly the case with regard to an Act of Parliament, which requires a more lengthy process than regulations. An Act of Parliament has to stand for a long time: the opportunity for an amendment is strictly limited and can usually only be done by or in another Act. Parliamentary time is rationed and a new Act will be deemed appropriate only if Ministers can demonstrate a pressing need to their colleagues. Relatively minor changes therefore have to wait until they can be incorporated in a major revision or included into a new Act referring to a related subject.

Whether primary or subordinate legislation is involved, the factors initiating change are broadly similar. A number of the significant factors are discussed here, together with a brief outline of the ways in which pressure for change is applied.

Timelag since establishment of existing controls

Food legislation is largely designed and drafted to be applied over a relatively long period of time. However, it is recognized that fixed legislation will become progressively outdated. Relatively minor points can be dealt with by means of amendments to the existing legislation but eventually the number of amendments causes the legislation to become unwieldy and potentially confusing. When this stage is reached, two options exist for improving the situation:

1. The existing legislation, together with all applicable amendments, can be consolidated without adding any new clauses. (The *Food Act, 1984*[1] is an example of such a consolidation); or
2. The legislation may be redrafted, including new clauses and provisions to make it more relevant to the current situation.

For certain of the subordinate legislation, revisions are required from time to time to take account of developments in food science and technology: the periodic reassessments of the legislation applying to the use of the various classes of food additive are appropriate examples.

Industry pressure

Legislation, by definition, limits the range of options available and although the presence of effective food legislation protects the 'honest trader' from unfair competition from those wishing to offer substandard goods, it can also prevent the adoption of novel processing techniques or limit the development of certain new products. Whenever this occurs to a significant extent, the food industry will seek to persuade government that a change is desirable.

Lobbying is generally undertaken on a sectoral basis by the appropriate trade association or, if the issue is applicable to all sectors of the food industry, by the Food and Drink Federation. (The topic of lobbying will be returned to later, page 118).

Consumer pressure

In many ways, consumer pressure may be viewed as being applied at the diametrically opposite point to industry pressure. The major objective is to instigate (or modify) measures which will control the activities of the food industry (for example, by limiting the use of specific named substances, or by establishing a particular compositional standard, or by preventing the use of specific processes) or require the provision of more information about their products.

Pressure from enforcement

Legislation can be effective only if it is capable of being enforced. The task of the enforcement bodies, principally the trading standards officers working for local government, is to ensure compliance and to monitor those instances where industry is able to circumvent the provisions of existing legislation. In addition, the processes of consumer protection activity enable the enforcement bodies to identify areas where the lack of formal controls can lead to inadequate protection for the consumer. In such instances the enforcement bodies will call for changes to the legislation. Such calls are generally made through the professional associations such as the Institute of Trading Standards Administration, or the Local Authorities Coordinating Body on Trading Standards (LACOTS), or the Environmental Health Officers Association.

Often, local authorities will act through their associations (the Association of County Councils or the Association of Metropolitan Authorities) as the democratically elected local Councillors will be closely in touch with the local consumer concerns and have the immediate advice of enforcement officers.

Recommendations from advisory bodies

Government is advised by a wide variety of advisory bodies, each of which produce detailed and specific recommendations. Advisory bodies exist to provide Ministers with an independent assessment of a specific topic or group of topics. Some bodies are constituted on a long-term basis and will report on a variety of issues. Other bodies are appointed on a short-term basis to provide advice on a single issue. All advisory bodies are limited in their deliberations to those subjects upon which Ministers have requested advice. Members of advisory committees are appointed on a personal basis and members are drawn from a wide variety of relevant disciplines and organizations. Certain committees (principally the Food Advisory Committee) are concerned directly with issues relating to food legislation while others, such as the Committee on Medical Aspects of Food Policy (COMA), have a less direct input into food legislation. For example, the 1984 COMA report on *Diet and Cardiovascular Disease*[2] recommended that foodstuffs be labelled with fat contents in order to assist consumers to be able to reduce fat consumption; this recommendation served to initiate government consideration of fat labelling.

Recommendations from parliamentary bodies

Parliamentary Select Committees in the course of their deliberations may make recommendations for changes to legislation. In addition, the Committee's reports contain verbatim accounts of the evidence presented to them; this evidence may also draw Ministers' attention to a need for new or revised legislation.

As with the advisory bodies referred to earlier, Select Committees operate within constraints laid down by government, although these are by no means as restrictive in the subjects to be covered. Select Committee reports are often critical of government, particularly with regard to technical matters rather than questions of policy. In general, the choice of subject investigated by a Select Committee tends to reflect the members' hope of influencing government by placing an issue on to the political agenda.

A recent example of a Select Committee examining food issues is provided by the House of Lords Select Committee on the European Communities. The Committee included in its report[3] for the session 1985–86, comments on food labelling, food additives, food contaminants and food irradiation.

Select Committee reports are advisory only; government retains full discretion on implementation.

The European Economic Community

Since UK accession to the EEC in 1973, Community initiatives have become a major factor, with several pieces of subordinate legislation arising from steps taken to harmonize food standards across the EEC. Implementation of EEC directives requires the establishment of specific provisions within UK legislation. The *Jam and Similar Products Regulations, 1981*[4] (referred to earlier) provide an example of UK food regulations being derived from a Community initiative. The impact of the EEC is considered in greater detail in Chapter 7.

The above list is by no means exhaustive but illustrates the major sources of pressure for change. In practice, pressure is often applied by several groups simultaneously as each identifies the need for change.

The strategies employed by those seeking a change in food legislation (be it primary or subordinate) generally include a number of major features:

1. Press coverage of the issue;
2. Direct communication with the Ministers and their departments;
3. Involvement of Members of Parliament who may be persuaded to ask suitable questions of the Minister in Parliament.

The objective at this stage is to convince Ministers that the subject is worthy of further examination. In practice, much food legislation has been of a relatively subjective nature and thus the aim has been to convince the government's advisers within the Ministry of Agriculture, Fisheries and Food that change is desirable in the public interest. The officials will convey the perceived need for change to their political masters.

Once the government has been convinced that there is potentially a need to establish or change food legislation, there are two distinct routes to be followed, depending on whether primary or subordinate legislation is under consideration. The next two chapters outline the main features of each route.

References

1. *Food Act, 1984* Eliz 2 (1984 ch 30). HMSO, London. 1984
2. Department of Health and Social Security *Diet and Cardiovascular Disease: Report of the Panel on Diet in Relation to Cardiovascular Disease. Committee on Medical Aspects of Food Policy.* Report on Health and Social Subjects No 28. HMSO, London. 1984
3. *Internal Market for Foodstuffs: 13th Report of the House of Lords Select Committee on the European Communities* HL (1985-86) 166. HMSO, London. 1986
4. *Jam and Similar Products Regulations, 1981* SI No 1063. HMSO, London. 1981

Replacing primary legislation

Once Ministers have been convinced that a prima-facie case exists for examining in more detail the necessity of amending or replacing the primary food legislation (such as *The Food Act, 1984*[1]) they will seek advice from various authorities. A departmental committee may be established to examine the issues for which change has been proposed. Discussion documents outlining options for change may be prepared and circulated to interested parties for comment. (For example, a 99-page discussion document[2] outlining possible changes to the *Food Act, 1984* was circulated in December 1984 with a six-month period allowed for comment). The civil servants involved will subsequently report to the Minister and if a case has been made for change and the Minister accepts that the issue merits further attention, the formal process towards a new Act will begin.

The discussion document of December 1984 is, in fact, a second attempt significantly to amend the primary food legislation. An earlier attempt during the late 1970s was abandoned at this stage without the publication of any official explanation. This fact alone illustrates the difficulties of initiating change and the reluctance of Ministers to find Parliamentary time for renewal of the primary legislation. However, from time to time, new primary legislation will be deemed to be desirable. The following paragraphs outline the principal stages through which a Bill is processed by Parliament. The description is given in general terms and, as such, applies to all Bills, no matter their subject. (The term 'Bill' as in *XYZ Bill* is used at all stages until Royal Assent is given, at which time the name changes to Act — as in *XYZ Act*.) *Table 5.1* illustrates the process by summarizing the timetable of events for the *Food Act, 1984* while *Table 5.2* provides a similar summary for the *Food and Environmental Protection Act, 1985*[3].

A key point to note from the two chronologies presented is the fact that whereas the *Food and Environment Bill* was steered through Parliament by Ministers representing the Ministry of Agriculture, Fisheries and Food, the *Food Bill* was taken through Parliament by the Government's chief legal officers, the Lord Chancellor in the Lords and the Attorney General in the Commons. This reflects the fact that the *Food Bill* was introduced solely to tidy numerous pieces of existing legislation into a single consolidated Act of Parliament and did not introduce any new provisions, whereas the *Food and Environment Protection Bill* includes a substantial number of new provisions.

Table 5.1   Chronology of the Food Act, 1984

Date	Stage	Hansard reference
12 Feb 84	Lord Hailsham (the Lord Chancellor) introduces Bill in House of Lords. First reading	HL Vol. 448 col. 1042
6 Mar 84	Lord Hailsham proposes Bill be read a second time. No debate. Referred to Joint Committee on Consolidation Bills. Views given in 7th Report for 1983–4 [HL 175]	HL Vol. 449 col. 145
10 May 84	No amendments proposed and no Lords wishing to speak in Committee. No debate. Order of recommitment discharged	HL Vol. 451 col. 1026
22 May 84	Third Reading. No debate. Bill passed and sent to Commons	HL Vol. 452 col. 145
8 Jun 84	Sir Michael Havers (The Attorney General) introduced Bill to Commons. No debate. Second reading	HC 61 col. 549
15 Jun 84	Considered in Committee. One minor technical amendment. Formal Third Reading. Bill passed with one amendment.	HC 61 col. 1197
21 Jun 84	House of Lords considers Commons amendment	HL Vol. 453 col. 440
26 Jun 84	Royal Assent	

Table 5.2   Chronology of the Food and Environment Protection Act, 1985

Date	Stage	Hansard reference
7 Nov 84	Lord Belstead (Minister of State, MAFF) introduces Bill in House of Lords. First reading	HL Vol. 457, col. 25
22 Nov 84	Lord Belstead opens debate on Bill. Bill read a second time. Committed to Committee of the whole House	HL Vol. 457 col. 697–738
6 Dec 84	Committee Stage – whole House, Bill debated clause by clause	HL Vol. 457 col. 1456–1463 HL Vol. 457 col. 1470–1507

Date	Stage	Hansard reference
		HL Vol. 457 col. 1512–1545
10 Dec 84	Committee Stage continued	HL Vol. 458 col. 127–139
22 Jan 85	Report Stage.	HL Vol. 459 col. 112–125
	Bill again considered clause by clause	HL Vol. 459 col. 133–212
5 Feb 85	Third Reading. Debate on general principles. Bill passed and sent to Commons.	HL Vol. 459 col. 1014–1054
5 Mar 85	John MacGregor MP (Minister of State, MAFF) opens debate on Bill in Commons. Second reading	HC Vol. 74 col. 795–860
19 Mar 85 to 30 Apr 85	Bill considered by Standing Committee (Minutes of proceedings published as [HC 364] 1984–85)	—
10 Jun 85	Report Stage. Standing Committee amendments considered. Two new clauses read first time, debated and read second time.	HC Vol. 80 col. 687–728
15 Jun 85	Report Stage continued. Followed by formal Third Reading. Bill passed with amendments.	HC Vol. 81 col. 922–969
12 Jul 85	House of Lords considers Commons amendments	HL Vol. 466 col. 428–444
16 Jul 85	Royal Assent	

Stages in processing a Bill

The first stage in the process of a Bill into law is to draft an initial version of the new bill which will be presented by the Minister to Cabinet and proposed to form part of the government's legislative programme.

The actual drafting of the wording of the Bill is undertaken by professionals working in the Office of Parliamentary Counsel on the instruction of the responsible department of government. The responsible department (MAFF in the case of most food legislation) — and ultimately the responsible Minister — decide the policy aspects to be included, while it is the draftsman's duty to take account of all matters relating to format and law.

Once drafted, the Bill is subjected to the full sequence of parliamentary procedure, including debate and consideration by committees. Most Bills are considered first by the House of Commons where the bulk of the political considerations relating to the Bill will be debated at length; subsequently, the Bill passes to the House of Lords for further consideration. Bills of a less contentious nature (including those relating to food) may be read first in the Lords and subsequently in the Commons. This arrangement serves to utilize scarce Parliamentary time most efficiently.

Introduction and first reading

The first reading is a purely formal matter: the Minister hands a 'dummy' of the Bill to the Clerk of the House. The Clerk reads the short title of the Bill and a date is announced for the second reading. No debate takes place at this stage and no explanation is given of the Bill's content.

The first printing of the Bill takes place at this point.

Second reading

At this stage the Bill is introduced to Parliament in some detail and is debated, concluding in a vote. The main objective at this stage is to consider the principle of the Bill and much of the debate centres on the necessity for the Bill and on the major themes included in or, indeed, excluded from, the Bill. The division (vote) generally gives agreement to the Bill's progress along the path to law.

Committee stage

The Bill is considered in detail, clause by clause during this stage, by a committee of Members of Parliament. The Bill may be amended but amendments at this stage do not alter the principle of the Bill, neither do they alter the government's proposals drastically.

The Committee stage may be completed very quickly in a single session or may extend over several weeks, depending on the length and complexity of the Bill and the degree to which its proposals are considered controversial. A consolidating Bill such as that which led to the *Food Act, 1984* requires less consideration than one introducing new elements to the law. Once the committee has concluded its deliberations, the Chairman 'reports' to the House. The Bill is then reprinted with the amendments which have been agreed.

Report stage

At this stage the Bill is considered by the House of Commons as a whole. As with the Committee stage, the Bill is considered clause by clause and amendments made. Minor amendments may be accepted without debate but most will be debated and voted upon.

Ministers (and other members of Parliament) often take advantage of this stage to introduce new clauses to a Bill. New clauses may be initiated in response to representations made to Ministers or be required due to developments in Government policies.

The Bill is again reprinted with amendments.

Third reading

The general principles of the Bill are debated again at this stage and, if still opposed, a vote is taken at the end of the debate. If approved, the Clerk of the House is ordered to deliver the Bill to the Lords. In practice, once a Bill reaches this stage it is virtually certain to become law.

House of Lords

The House of Lords will consider the Bill, following the same basic stages, but usually progression through the Lords is achieved with greater speed. The Lords may amend the Bill in the same way as described earlier for the Commons.

Lords' Amendment

Amendments made in the Lords are considered in turn by the Commons. Most are accepted, although from time to time a compromise position must be achieved.

This point completes the parliamentary consideration of the Bill. The Bill is held by the Clerk of the Parliaments until the ceremony at which Royal Assent takes place.

As was stated earlier and may be seen from the chronology presented for the *Food and Environment Protection Act, 1985*, a Bill may be read first in the House of Lords with the House of Commons consideration following the third reading in the Lords. Parliamentary attention ends with the Lords considering Commons' amendments rather than vice versa.

Royal Assent

Royal Assent is generally given by the Lords' Commissioners on behalf of the Queen at a ceremony held at the Bar of the House of Lords. At this point the Bill becomes an Act of Parliament.

After the Royal Assent, an Act may come into force immediately or may be introduced after a period of time. The *Food Act, 1984*, for example, received Royal Assent on 26 June 1984 but did not come into force until 26 September 1984. In certain instances an Act may be brought into force over a period of time, with different sections applying from different dates.

The main points to note about the sequence of events outlined above are the many opportunities given for support or opposition to be voiced by any Member of Parliament who wishes to do so. Acts, as primary legislation, are intended to serve for a significant period of time and thus the content is considered in depth. A major strength of the system is the published nature of the parliamentary process with debates being recorded in Hansard, reported in the media and thus open to public scrutiny.

Primary legislation relating to foodstuffs is generally not subject to replacement each time government changes, which characterizes much legislation of a more party political nature. For this reason, food legislation generally has a long life, being replaced from time to time by means of consolidation to incorporate intervening amendments.

Such a replacement has a straightforward passage through the system because consolidation is an uncontroversial procedure, conducted only when timely and convenient. Substantive changes requiring a completely new Bill or new provisions follow the full procedures described above. Legislation is therefore replaced or updated only when it is generally agreed that any new provisions are necessary. This means that any possibility of a radical rethink of the provisions of the *Food Act, 1984* represents a once-in-a-generation opportunity to achieve change.

References

1. *Food Act, 1984* Eliz 2 (1984 ch 30). HMSO, London. 1984
2. Ministry of Agriculture, Fisheries and Food (Standards Division) *Review of Food Legislation*. Ministry of Agriculture, Fisheries and Food, London. December 1984
3. *Food and Environment Protection Act, 1985* Eliz 2 (1985 ch 48). HMSO, London. 1985

Making regulations

The process through which significant changes are made to subordinate legislation relating to food composition, labelling and processing follows a different route to that described for primary legislation. As the legislation is delegated in the *Food Act, 1984*[1] to Ministers, the main stages are not parliamentary (as with primary legislation) but are conducted within the government department concerned (generally, but not invariably, this is the Ministry of Agriculture, Fisheries and Food).

The process begins much as described earlier: a case has to be made supporting change. Once the Ministers have been convinced of the need for change, the officials prepare background papers on the topic in question, outlining the main points. These will include:

1. The existing regulatory provisions;
2. The reasons why the existing regulations are considered to be inadequate or otherwise worthy of review;
3. Options for future regulations.

Although the legislation is delegated to Ministers, they are constrained by the provisions of the *Food Act, 1984*, which require that the views of interested parties be taken into account:

> Before making any regulation . . . the Ministers shall consult with such organisations as appear to them to be representative of interests substantially affected by the regulations

(*Food Act, 1984* section 118)

A point to note here is the use of the word 'organizations'. There is no statutory obligation for departments or Ministers to consult with individuals or even with individual firms; however, in practice, any evidence provided by an individual or an individual firm will be taken into account, together with information provided by organizations. There are a number of ways in which such consultations may take place and, in most reviews, interested parties are given several opportunities to make their views known.

Advisory committees

For many issues, the Ministers will seek advice from one or more of the advisory committees which exist for this purpose.

The Food Advisory Committee

At present the major advisory committee in this context is the Food Advisory Committee (FAC). This committee's role is as follows:

> To advise the Minister of Agriculture, Fisheries and Food, the Secretary of State for Social Services, the Secretary of State for Wales, the Secretary of State for Scotland and the Head of the Department of Health and Social Services for Northern Ireland on matters referred to it by Ministers relating to:
>
> (a) The composition, labelling and advertising of food.
> (b) Additives, contaminants and other substances which are, or may be, present in food or used in its preparation;
>
> with particular reference to the exercise of powers conferred on Ministers by Sections 4, 5 and 7 of the *Food Act, 1984* and the corresponding provisions in enactments relating to Scotland and Northern Ireland[2].

Ministers have for many years been advised on significant changes to food regulations by advisory committees. In its report, in 1896, the Select Committee on Food Products Adulteration recommended that a Court of Reference be established to advise on definitions and standards for various foods[3]. This recommendation was not taken up and for many years advice was sought from groups specifically brought together to consider a particular issue. The present system, which involves a permanently constituted advisory committee, may be traced historically to 1931 when a committee under the Minister for Health was set up to advise whether changes were necessary in the system of obtaining advice on food matters. The committee reported to Parliament in 1934 and its report was published in 1938[4]. During its deliberations the committee received evidence from a variety of bodies including food manufacturing industry, and food law enforcement bodies (local authorities, public analysts). The Society of Public Analysts (SPA) recommended that a permanent body with no other duties be established to reconcile the views of the many parties interested in food standards. The Minister's committee rejected this advice and considered that such a body was not necessary. However, with the need for tighter control of food during the Second World War, an Interdepartmental Committee (which included members of the SPA as well as civil servants from the Ministry of Food, Ministry of Health, Department of Health for Scotland and the Laboratory of the Government Chemist) was set up in 1942 to advise the Minister of Food. From this body the Food Standards Committee (FSC) was formed in 1947.

The function of the FSC was similar to that of the present FAC:

> To advise the Ministers of Food and Health and the Secretary of State for Scotland as to the provisions to be made concerning the composition of foods (other than liquid milk) and the labelling and marking of any foods for which provision is made, by:
>
> (a) Statutory orders under the Defence (Sale of Food) Regulations; or
>
> (b) Regulations (other than Milk or Dairy Regulations) under the Food and Drugs Acts and corresponding enactments relating to Scotland;
>
> for preventing danger to health, loss of nutritional value or otherwise protecting purchasers.[5]

The FSC included industry representatives (appointed in a personal capacity), academics and consumers in the decision-making process. Initially, the FSC was chaired by the Chief Scientific Adviser to the Ministry of Food (later Chief Scientific Adviser (Food) MAFF) but from 1959 the committee was chaired by individuals independent of the law-making Ministries. In 1951, a subcommittee was established to consider the use of preservatives in food. The subcommittee's brief was subsequently expanded to include all additives and contaminants, and in 1963 was reconstituted as the Food Additives and Contaminants Committee (FACC). The FACC was given the task of providing a sound basis of control for food additive use and undertook a systematic review of each class of additive with the aim of limiting the use of additives to permitted lists.

The FACC terms of reference were as follows:

> To advise the Minister of Agriculture, Fisheries and Food, the Secretary of State for Scotland, the Minister for Health, and as respects Northern Ireland, the Secretary of State for the Home Department on matters referred to them by Ministers in relation to food contaminants, additives and similar substances which are or may be present in food, or used in its preparation, with particular reference to the exercise of powers conferred on Ministers by Sections 4, 5 and 7 of the Food and Drugs Act, 1955 and the corresponding provisions in enactments relating to Scotland and Northern Ireland.[6]

With regard to food additives, the key question considered by the FACC (and today by the FAC) was that of need. The responsibility for assessing safety-related evidence lies elsewhere. There is an established policy that any advice relating to safety is not sought until the case for need has been established; this arrangement serves to reduce the workload of those assessing safety, as there is clearly no benefit to be gained from assessing the safety of a substance for which no need can be demonstrated. The question of need is central to past and present legislation relating to food additive use. Section 4(2) of the *Food Act, 1984* requires that

Ministers shall have regard to the desirability of restricting, as far as practicable, the use of substances of no nutritional value as foods or as ingredients in foods.

In order to assess whether a genuine need exists, the FACC evolved a set of general criteria which are still in operation today. The application for any new additive must provide 'evidence that there is a clear benefit to the consumer that cannot reasonably be achieved by use of an already permitted additive, or by any other means'[7]. This principle was also applied by the FACC in the course of its systematic review of the additives already permitted in the various classes. A full list of published reports produced by the FSC is given as *Table 6.1* and a list of FACC reports given as *Table 6.2*.

Table 6.1   Food Standards Committee Reports

Report No.	Date	Subject
FSC/REP/77	1983	Mince
FSC/REP/76	1982	Cream
FSC/REP/75	1982	Cheese
FSC/REP/74	1981	Magarine and other table spreads
FSC/REP/73	1981	Infant formulae
FSC/REP/72	1980	Meat products
FSC/REP/71	1980	Claims/misleading descriptions
FSC/REP/70	1978	Water in food
FSC/REP/69	1979	Labelling
FSC/REP/69b	1979	Exceptions from ingredient listing and generic labelling
FSC/REP/69a	1979	Use of fructose in food specially prepared for diabetics
FSC/REP/68	1977	Beer
FSC/REP/67	1976	Change from calorie to joule in food energy descriptions
FSC/REP/66	1976	EEC Draft Directive on fruit jams, jellies, marmalade and chestnut puree
FSC/REP/65	1976	Soft drinks
FSC/REP/64	1975	Yogurt
FSC/REP/63	1975	Fruit juices
FSC/REP/62	1975	Novel proteins
FSC/REP/61	1974	Bread and flour
FSC/REP/60	1973	Condensed milk
FSC/REP/59	1972	Date marking of foods
FSC/REP/58	1971	Vinegar
FSC/REP/57	1971	Date marking of foods (interim report)
FSC/REP/56	1970	Offals in meat products
FSC/REP/55	1970	Pre 1955 compositional orders
FSC/REP/54	1969	Condensed milk
FSC/REP/53	1969	Jam and other preserves
FSC/REP/52	1968	Soups
FSC/REP/51	1967	Cream
FSC/REP/50	1966	Claims and misleading descriptions
FSC/REP/49	1965	Fish and meat pastes
FSC/REP/48	1964	Food labelling
FSC/REP/47	1963	Meat pie
FSC/REP/46	1962	Canned meat

FSC/REP/45	1962	Dried milk
FSC/REP/44	1962	Hard, soft and cream cheese
FSC/REP/43	1960	Bread and flour
FSC/REP/42	1959	Milk bread
FSC/REP/41	Not Publ	Starch syrup in table jellies
FSC/REP/40	1959	Soft drinks
FSC/REP/39	1957	Ice cream standard
FSC/REP/38	1956	Processed cheese and cheese spread
FSC/REP/37	1956	Sausages
FSC/REP/36	1954	Vitaminisation of margarine
FSC/REP/35	1952	Jam and marmalade
FSC/REP/34	Not Publ	Coffee mixture
FSC/REP/33	1952	Shredded suet and block suet
FSC/REP/32	1952	Saccharine and other sweetening tablets
FSC/REP/31	Not Publ	Fish cakes
FSC/REP/30	1951	Artificial cream
FSC/REP/29	1951	Synthetic cream
FSC/REP/28	Not Publ	Edible gelatine
FSC/REP/27	Not Publ	Soft drinks
FSC/REP/26	1951	Coffee mixture
FSC/REP/25	1951	Fish cakes
FSC/REP/24	Not Publ	Ice cream (suppl)
FSC/REP/23	1950	Cream
FSC/REP/22	Not Publ	Ice cream
FSC/REP/21	1950	Fish paste
FSC/REP/20	1949	Edible gelatine
FSC/REP/19	1948	Iodized salt
FSC/REP/18	1948	Processed cheese
FSC/REP/17	1948	Curry powder
FSC/REP/16	1948	Tomato ketchup
FSC/REP/15*	1946	Fluorine
FSC/REP/14	1945	Self raising flour
FSC/REP/13	1945	Salad cream and mayonnaise
FSC/REP/12	1945	Custard powder
FSC/REP/11	1944	Coffee essence
FSC/REP/10	1943	Dripping and tallow
FSC/REP/9	1943	Vinegar
FSC/REP/8	1943	Shredded suet
FSC/REP/7	1943	Mustard
FSC/REP/6	1943	Baking powder and golden raising powder
FSC/REP/5	1943	Soft drinks
FSC/REP/4	1942	Self raising flour
FSC/REP/3	1942	Coffee essence
FSC/REP/2	1942	Soya in sausage (suppl)
FSC/REP/1	1942	Soya in sausage

* 1 – 15 by Interdepartmental Committee set up by Ministry of Food. Reports 16 onwards by Food Standards Committee.

Table 6.2   Reports on food additives and contaminants
(a)   By the Food Additives and Contaminants Committee

Subject	Date
Arsenic in foods	1984
Metals in canned foods	1983
—	Not publ
—	Not publ
Enzyme preparations	1982
Sweeteners	1982
—	Not publ
Baking aids	1980
Modified starches	1980
Asbestos in relation to food and drink	1979
Colouring matters	1979
Flavour modifiers	1978
Nitrites & nitrates in cured meats and cheese	1978
Additives in beer	1978
Solvents	1978
Sorbic acid	1977
—	Not publ
Flavourings	1976
Lead in food	1975
Mineral hydrocarbons	1975
Liquid freezants	1974*
Antioxidants	1974
Solvents	1974
Emulsifiers and stabilizers	1972*
Liquid freezants	1972
Preservatives	1972
Additives in bread and flour	1971*
Antioxidants	1971*
Packaging	1970
Emulsifiers and stabilizers	1970
Azodicarbonamide	1968
Further classes of additives	1968
Cyclamates	1967
Aldrin and dieldrin	1967
Antioxidants	1966*
Cyclamates	1966
Solvents	1966
Antioxidants	1965*

(b)   By the Food Standards Committee

Subject	Date
Flavouring agents	1965
Colouring matters	1964
Antioxidants	1963
Limits for arsenic and lead in yeast and yeast products	Not publ
Mineral oil in food	1962
Citrus red	Not publ
Preservatives in food	Not publ
Preservatives in food	1959
Fluorine	1957
Emulsifying and stabilizing agents	1956

Copper	1956
Colouring matters	1955
Arsenic	1955
Colouring matters	1955
Lead	1954
Antimony and cadmium	Not publ
Antioxidants	1954
Zinc	1954*
Antioxidants	1953
Fluorine	1953
Tin in canned food	1952*
Copper	1951
Lead	1951
Arsenic	1951
Arsenic	1950

* Most reports have been published by Her Majesty's Stationery Office. Reports marked *
available from Ministry of Agriculture, Fisheries and Food.

By the early 1980s the FACC had virtually completed its review of the various categories of additive and in 1983 the FSC and FACC were merged to form the Food Advisory Committee (FAC). Reports from the FAC are listed in *Table 6.3*. Like its predecessors, the FAC is an independent non-expert group: committee members are appointed on a personal basis and thus are not (as such) representatives of organizations. Members are drawn from the food industry, the Association of Public Analysts, trading standards bodies, medical professions, academic institutions, research organizations and organizations representing consumers. When new members are appointed to the Committee, there is an overt attempt to achieve a broad variety of experience and when the FAC membership was revised in November 1986, the spectrum of advice was broadened with an extra member with consumer affairs experience and, for the first time, a member with expertise in food retailing[8]. A list of the current members of the FAC is provided in each of the Committee's reports. At the time of writing (1987) the membership is constituted as follows: seven from the food and related industries; two consumer representatives; two from clinical medicine; two directors of research institutes, and two from the bodies responsible for the enforcement of food legislation (*Table 6.4*).

The FAC reports to Ministers (as above) and is serviced by both scientific and administrative officials from the Food Science and Stan-

Table 6.3   Food Advisory Committee Reports

Report No.	Date	Subject
FdAC/REP/1	1984	Skimmed milk with non-milk fat regulations 1960*
FdAC/REP/2	1985	Use of additives to cloud soft drinks*
FdAC/REP/3	1987	Coated and ice-glazed fish products**
FdAC/REP/4	1987	Colouring matter in food regulations 1973**

* Published by Ministry of Agriculture, Fisheries and Food
** Published by HMSO

Table 6.4   Food Advisory Committee Membership

Name	Affiliation
Professor Frank Curtis	Director of the Agricultural and Food Research Council's Food Research Institute, Norwich
Dr Margaret Ashwell	Principal of the Good Housekeeping Institute
Mrs Anne Ballard	General Secretary to the Federation of Women's Institutes
Mr Michael Boxall	Company Secretary, Tesco PLC
Dr Howard Eggins	Director of Bioquest Ltd
Dr Bill Fulton	Senior Technical Member of the Food and Drinks Co-ordination Management Group, Unilever Ltd
Dr Tom Gorsuch	Director of Research and Quality Control. Colmans of Norwich
Mr Tony Harrison	Chief Scientific Adviser, Public Analyst and Official Agricultural Analyst, Avon and Gloucestershire County Councils
Professor Phillip James	Director of Rowett Research Institute
Miss Patricia Mann	Head of External Affairs, J. Walter Thompson Group
Mr Roger Manley	Controller of Trading Standards, Cheshire County Council
Mr Tony Skrimshire	General Manager, Research Development and Quality Assurance, H. J. Heinz Company Ltd
Mr Alan Turner	Recently Retired Chief Chemist, Cadbury Schweppes PLC
Professor Paul Turner	Professor of Clinical Pharmacology St Bartholomew's Hospital, and Chairman of the Committee on Toxicity of Chemicals in Food, Consumer Products and the Environment
Dr Elspeth R Young	Senior Registrar (p.t.) in Dermatology, Wycombe General Hospital and the John Radcliffe Hospital, Oxford

Source: MAFF Press Release. December 1986

dards Divisions of MAFF. In addition, there is direct opportunity for the Department of Health and Social Security to advise, particularly with regard to aspects relating to food safety and public health.

In addition to the officials referred to above, the FAC may call upon the assistance of technical advisers either from elsewhere in the public service or from industry. Such technical advisers are appointed on an *ad hoc* basis and provide expertise relevant to a particular enquiry. For example, Professor G. C. Cheeseman, formerly the head of the Processing Division at the National Institute for Research in Dairying, served as expert assessor when the Food Standards Committee reviewed cream and cheese in the early 1980s[9,10].

The FAC, like its predecessors the FSC and the FACC, is given a specific brief by the Ministers and its reviews are limited to this brief. The committee is not free to select its own topics, although it may make recommendations for further review. Once a review has been initiated, the committee calls for interested bodies to submit such evidence as is appropriate to the topic under review. The announcement of a review is by means of a government press release which may be taken up by the interested trade press and (much more rarely) by the general media. Organizations identified as having a particular interest in the topic are specifically invited to contribute evidence, while other bodies are notified by an announcement which is mailed to those on the Ministry's mailing list.

The review process is, in theory, open to submissions from a very wide variety of groups; in practice, for most topics, the overwhelming proportion of submissions to FAC reviews have been from industry and enforcement groups. The range of submissions is possibly limited by the fact that the reviews are not always 'newsworthy', and many individuals or organizations with potentially relevant information are therefore likely to be unaware of the review and the procedures for submitting evidence.

The Committee considers the background papers, the written submissions and assessments from other bodies. On rare occasions, certain key groups may be invited to present evidence to the committee orally and this occasion may be used to provide the members with the opportunity to test out ideas which may subsequently be incorporated in the final report to the Ministers.

Throughout the Committee's deliberations, an underlying aim is for it to achieve a consensus viewpoint which may be published. One principle, identified by a former chairman of the FSC, is that:

> in the long term, there can be no fundamental divergence of interest between the consumer and the industries which supply him with his food. The food manufacturing industry must satisfy the desires, preferences and nutritional needs of the consumer.[11]

As stated earlier, the role of the FAC is to advise and, to this end, reports from the FAC (and other advisory committees) include detailed and specific recommendations.

In due course, the FAC presents its report to Ministers and it may be published. The general format of a report is as follows:

1. Statement of scope of review;
2. Reasons for review;
3. Discussion of market for food under review;
4. Current legislation;
5. Suggested need for control;
6. Discussion of compositional matters;
7. Discussion of labelling issues;
8. Discussion of issues relating to additives etc;
9. Summary of recommendations;
10. Appendices containing technical information or reports from working parties (e.g. on nutrition, toxicology or analytical aspects).

The report generally includes a list of all those organizations which have contributed evidence, although the representations remain private.

A degree of controversy about the question of the application of the *Official Secrets Act, 1911*[12] to materials provided to members of advisory committees has grown up in recent years and it is worth clarifying the situation. On 16 May 1986 it was stated in Parliament that, although committee members are not required to sign any form of declaration

> the *Official Secrets Act* applies to all official information whether or not a declaration has been signed[13].

On 9 July 1986, answering a question specifically relating to the Food Advisory Committee, Mrs Peggy Fenner said:

> Members of the Food Advisory Committee are told on appointment that where appropriate they must observe the confidentiality of information passed to them as part of their duties on that committee. It is the *Official Secrets Act* that makes it an offence to disclose such information without authority[14].

No doubt the subject of public access to submissions made to the FAC and other government advisory committees will continue to be addressed. In the longer term, a shift in government policy on this matter may result in change in the extent of public access. Meanwhile, the committee does not publish the details of any representations although they may be referred to in the body of the committee's report. Advisory committees, however, seek to encourage the publication of all data relating to the *safety* of a product or ingredient which has been provided in support of a submission and where for any reason this data is not easily accessible. For example, in Appendix II of the 1982 FACC *Report on the Review of Sweeteners in Food*, the Committee on Toxicology wrote

> We are concerned that much of the information considered has not been published and we would reiterate our comments made in an earlier report that all toxicological information on food additives should be published in reputable journals to enable the results to be assessed critically by the scientific community[15].

However, it is recognized that there may be difficulties in getting more material published because of the quantity of routine material involved. Publication is particularly desirable when issues would otherwise be considered solely on the basis of private and generally confidential toxicological evidence submitted by a manufacturer. In recognition of this concern, MAFF has recently altered its procedures to enable a *bona fide* enquirer to have access to safety-related toxicological information submitted to its Advisory Committees. MAFF now require the person holding copyright to place a copy of the information for reference at the British Library. This development relates solely to those matters relating to safety, which have previously been discussed on the basis of information not generally available. The proposal does not yet extend to include all evidence submitted to advisory committees.

Although the FAC is the principal advisory committee with regard to food compositional and labelling standards, other committees also exist to provide Ministers with specific advice on matters which relate to the safety of foods and other aspects relevant to the nation's food policy.

Other advisory bodies

At this stage it is worth briefly introducing a number of the main advisory bodies, each of which operates in a manner broadly similar to the FAC.

The Committee on Toxicology of Chemicals in Food, Consumer Products and the Environment (COT)

This Committee, initially known as the toxicity subcommittee of the Committee on Medical Aspects of Chemicals in Food and the Environment, has the following general terms of reference:

1. At the request of Government Departments to assess and advise on the toxic risk to man of substances which are:

    (a) used or proposed to be used as food additives, or used in such a way that they might contaminate food through their use or natural occurrence in agriculture, including horticulture and veterinary practice, or in the distribution, storage, preparation, processing or packaging of food;
    (b) used or proposed to be used or manufactured or produced in industry, agriculture, food storage or any other workplace;
    (c) used or proposed to be used as household goods or toilet goods and preparations;
    (d) used or proposed to be used as drugs, when advice is requested by the Medicines Committee, Section 4 Committees or the Licencing Authority;
    (e) used or proposed to be used or disposed of in such a way as to result in pollution of the environment.

2. To advise on important general principles of new scientific discoveries in connection with toxic risks, to co-ordinate with other bodies concerned with the assessment of toxic risks and to present recommendations for toxicity testing[16].

From the above terms of reference, it may be seen that this Committee has a wide-ranging function, of which considerations relating to food ingredients are but one aspect.

One of the Committee's major roles with regard to food is the assessment of safety-in-use of food additives. When a manufacturer seeks to gain approval for a substance to be used as an additive there is, first of all, an assessment of the need for such an additive by the FAC. As stated previously, only those substances for which a strong case for need has been made will have their toxicological safety assessed; all others are rejected without the necessity of COT review. The DHSS sets out guidelines for testing of chemicals for toxicity[17] (and for carcinogenicity[18] and mutagenicity[19], reviews of which are dealt with by other specialist committees), the results of which are submitted to support the case for the new additive. The data submitted are summarized before consideration by the Committee. This summary has traditionally been prepared independently by the scientific secretariat of the DHSS but, since 1986, government has suggested that to speed the progress of review it would be advantageous if the petitioner could prepare the summary and present it with the full and detailed report. Guidance on the preparation of summaries of data was published in 1986[20].

Once the COT has reviewed all the available evidence its report with references is published; usually this is as an appendix to a report from another committee such as FAC.

The Committee on Medical Aspects of Food Policy (COMA)

This Committee, chaired by the Chief Medical Officer, DHSS, advises government on a variety of topics relating to medical and nutritional aspects of food policy in Britain. Because of the variety of professional skills required to assess the evidence on the range of topics to be examined, COMA operates by appointing expert panels or working parties to review specific questions. Such groups are generally brought together to prepare a report (or series of reports) on a defined subject. Three examples are given below.

The Panel on Diet in Relation to Diet and Cardiovascular Disease. This panel, under the chairmanship of Professor Philip Randle, had the following terms of reference:

> To advise the Committee on Medical Aspects of Food Policy on the significance of the relation between nutrition and cardiovascular disease and to make recommendations.[21]

The panel was appointed at the end of 1981 and presented its report in 1984. One feature of the panel's report was that in addition to advising dietary change for the population, it also contained recommendations relating to the labelling of foods with an indication of fat content.

The Panel on Novel Foods. This panel has the following role:

1. To consider the nutritional recommendations made in the Food Standards Committee Report on Novel Protein Foods;
2. To consider any novel food submitted by manufacturers under scrutiny arrangements to be set up by the Ministry of Agriculture, Fisheries and Food;

3. To consider the nutritional aspects of novel foods and novel food processes.[22]

A recent role for this panel has been its contribution to the consideration relating to food irradiation (see later).

The Panel on Bread, Flour and other Cereal Products. This panel was established in 1978 and reported in 1981. Its terms of reference were as follows:

In the light of available medical and scientific evidence,

(a) to consider the nutritive value of bread, flour and other cereal products and their importance in the diet, and
(b) to make any appropriate recommendations.[23]

The above panels are included only as examples; the full list also includes groups advising government on child nutrition, nutrition of the elderly, the composition of foods for infants and young children, and nutritional surveillance.

During 1986 the main COMA committee recommended that a panel be established to examine the role of sugars in relation to health[24]. The new panel held its first meeting on 18 February 1987 under the chairmanship of Professor Harry Keen[25]. It is likely that the panel will base its deliberations on existing reviews of sugar and health (such as the 1986 report from the American Food and Drugs Administration[26]) rather than considering in detail each and every paper on the subject.

The Advisory Committee on Irradiated and Novel Foods (ACINF)

The terms of reference of this topic-specific advisory committee were as follows:

To advise Health and Agriculture Ministers of Great Britain and the Head of the Department of Health and Social Services for Northern Ireland on any matters relating to the irradiation of food or to the manufacture of novel foods or foods produced by novel processes, having regard where appropriate to the views of relevant expert bodies.

The committee reported its conclusions to government in a report published in April 1986.[27]

The Standing Panel on Hazards from Microbiological Contamination of Food

The terms of reference of this panel are:

To keep under review any hazards to the public health from the microbiological contamination of food sold or intended for sale for human consumption and to review processes to which the food may be subjected.[28]

Bodies indirectly concerned with food safety

Each of the bodies referred to above is primarily concerned with the maintenance of public health and thus each is serviced by DHSS officials although there is direct input from MAFF. However, in addition to those committees described above, each of which provides advice of direct relevance to food-related legislation, there are other committees, such as the Advisory Committee on Pesticides (ACP), which have an indirect role in the maintenance of food safety. The ACP role is to advise Ministers on the use of pesticides in much the same way that the FAC advises on the use of food additives. The operation of ACP parallels the Food Advisory Committee in many ways: for example, its referral of specialist matters to experts in particular topics. A scientific subcommittee is assisted by expert panels as follows:

1. Medical and toxicological;
2. Environment;
3. Labelling and container design;
4. Pesticide application technology.[29]

However, the ACP differs from the FAC in a number of key aspects:

1. Following the *Food and Environment Protection Act, 1985*[30], the ACP has been given a statutory role with its terms of reference set out in the Act (Section 16) and details of its operation specified (Schedule 5). The FAC, together with the other bodies described earlier, is non-statutory and Ministers are not *required* to seek its advice.
2. The FAC and the other food-related committees only review matters referred to them by Ministers. The ACP role is:

    to give them (Ministers) advice, either *when requested or otherwise on any matters* relating to the control of pests . . . Section 16(7) (emphasis added).

3. The ACP is required to present an annual report of its activities. The FAC is not required to produce such a report.
4. The membership of the ACP is drawn entirely from the public sector with members selected for their professional expertise in various medical sciences, biological sciences or analytical chemistry. By contrast, the FAC membership is drawn from a wider base and the FAC is thus a 'non-expert' body.

The functions of all the different advisory committees are broadly similar, as is their general method of operation which has been described above for the FAC. For many issues the committees interact, with one taking the lead role but seeking advice on specific aspects from the others. For example, when considering a food additive the FAC will concentrate primarily on aspects relating to need and will seek advice on toxicological matters from the Committee on Toxicology of Chemicals in Food, Consumer Products and the Environment

(COT). Similarly, the Advisory Committee on Irradiated and Novel Foods (ACINF) when considering the subject of food irradiation sought advice as follows:

1. From the FAC on matters relating to labelling;
2. From the COT on toxicology;
3. From the COMA Panel on Novel Foods on nutritional aspects;
4. From the Standing Panel on Hazards from Microbiological Contamination of Foods on microbiological aspects;
5. From the National Radiological Protection Board on the radiation aspects.

Each Committee's report is commissioned by Ministers and it is to Ministers that the report is presented via the appropriate Parliamentary Secretary. Reports are generally published, although Ministers may choose not to publish, or to delay publication. In 'normal' circumstances there is a delay of 6–9 months before an advisory committee's report is published, the exact length of time depending on the volume of material passing through Her Majesty's Stationery Office at the time. Most reports are given relatively low priority. Ministers have the power to delay publication further, but to do so may be unwise as the report's inception and progress is usually public knowledge: delay or non-publication could readily give rise to outcry. The great majority of reports have been published but, in more recent years, one or two minor reports have not been published via HMSO as is normal: rather they have been made available on request to the Ministry of Agriculture, Fisheries and Food[31].

Once an advisory committee's report has been presented to the Minister and published, there is further opportunity for interested parties to make their views known. The objective at this stage is to influence the course of action which will take place following the published recommendations.

Each committee's report presents recommendations to Ministers and these recommendations may or may not be accepted. The comments received, together with the published report, are used by officials to prepare a paper summarizing the comments, which is sent to the advisory committee who may choose to amend their recommendations in the light of new evidence. In the case of the FAC, this reference of submissions back to the committee is a strategy based on FACC method of operation rather than that of the FSC: the publication of a FSC report completed that committee's duties.

After the advisory committee

The committee's reports plus the comments received are used by officials to prepare advice for Ministers, and if a change in legislation is suggested and the need accepted by Ministers, then a document outlining the proposals is circulated to those on the Ministry's mailing list.

The circulation of documents at this and subsequent stages represents the formal consultations specifically required by Section 118 of the *Food Act, 1984* as distinct from the 'pre-formal' inputs to an advisory committee and to Ministers after publication of the committee's reports.

A further period is allowed for comments; subsequently, officials will again prepare advice to Ministers. These stages may be repeated one or more times as the proposals are refined in the light of critical comment. Officials will also seek specific comment from those most involved and will meet with representatives of industry and the enforcement bodies.

If a change in the regulations is still regarded as necessary, the legislative documentation will be drafted. Unlike the primary legislation which is drafted by a central body (the Office of the Parliamentary Counsel), subordinate legislation is drafted by the legal departments of the Ministry concerned.

Where significant discussion has taken place with regard to the regulatory provisions proposed, a further opportunity for comment is allowed for once the statutory instrument has been drafted. Discussions at this stage are confined to questions relating to the legal workability of the instrument and not to the central provisions as such.

The instrument is redrafted where necessary and presented to the Ministers for final signature. Once approved, the statutory instrument is 'laid' before Parliament. The procedure involves the delivery of the instrument to both the Votes and Proceedings Office of the House of Commons and the Office of the Clerk of the Parliaments. There is no general requirement for Parliamentary consideration, and the regulations come into force at a given date which, under normal circumstances, cannot be less than 21 days after the instrument is 'laid'; however, in extreme cases where there is a need to protect public health, this period may be reduced.

There is opportunity for Parliamentary consideration of new regulations by means of what is known as a negative resolution procedure. During the 40 sitting days after the instrument is 'laid', any member of Parliament may 'pray' against the new regulations by calling for a motion of annulment known as a 'prayer'. If such a motion is brought before Parliament there will be a debate followed by a division. If the prayer is successful, the new regulations will be revoked by means of an Order of Council. Prayers against regulations are unusual and are not generally successful.

It may be seen from the above sequence of events that once an advisory committee has reported, the bulk of subordinate food legislation is essentially considered in confidence between officials and 'interested parties', whereas the primary food legislation, like other primary legislation, is subject to (considerably more visible) Parliamentary procedures.

References

1. *Food Act, 1984* (1984 ch 30) HMSO, London. 1984
2. Ministry of Agriculture, Fisheries and Food *Additives No 2* Food Facts Information Sheet. Press Office, MAFF. December 1986

3. *Report of the Select Committee on Food Products Adulteration* House of Commons 1896 (288) IX (Reprinted in *British Parliamentary Papers: Health, Food and Drugs* Volume 4. Irish University Press, Shannon. 1969

4. Ministry of Health *Report of the Departmental Committee on the Composition and Description of Food* Cmd 4564. HMSO, London. 1938

5. Ward, A. G. *Advising on Food Standards in the United Kingdom: 1. The Changing Role of the Food Standards Committee.* In: Ministry of Agriculture, Fisheries and Food, *Food Quality and Safety: A Century of Progress. Proceedings of the Symposium celebrating the Centenary of the Sale of Food and Drugs Act, 1875.* HMSO, London. 1976

6. Cited in FACC Reports — see, for example: Ministry of Agriculture, Fisheries and Food *Food Additives and Contaminants Committee Report on the Review of Sweeteners in Food* FAC/REP/34. HMSO, London. 1982

7. Ministry of Agriculture, Fisheries and Food *Additives No 7* Food Facts Information Sheet. Press Office, MAFF. December 1986

8. MAFF op.cit. (reference 2).

9. Ministry of Agriculture, Fisheries and Food *Food Standards Committee Report on Cream* FSC/REP/76. HMSO, London. 1982

10. Ministry of Agriculture, Fisheries and Food *Food Standards Committee Report on Cheese* FSC/REP/75. HMSO, London. 1982

11. Ward, A. G. op.cit. (reference 5)

12. *Official Secrets Act, 1911* Geo 5 (1911 ch 28), HMSO, London. 1911

13. Hayhoe, Barney (Minister for Health). Written Answer to Laurie Pavitt. Question on Advisory Committees. *Hansard* 6th Series Vol 97 col 583. 16 May 1986

14. Fenner, Peggy (Parliamentary Secretary, Ministry of Agriculture, Fisheries and Food) Written Answer to Tony Lloyd. Question on the Food Advisory Committee. *Hansard* 6th Series Vol 101 col 196–197. 9 July 1986

15. MAFF op.cit. (reference 5)

16. As cited in: Department of Health and Social Security *Advisory Committee on Irradiated and Novel Foods. Report on the Safety and Wholesomeness of Irradiated Foods.* HMSO, London. 1986

17. Department of Health and Social Security *Guidelines for the Testing of Chemicals for Toxicity* Reports on Health and Social Subjects No. 27. HMSO, London. 1983

18. Department of Health and Social Security *Guidelines for the Testing of Chemicals for Carcinogenicity* Reports on Health and Social Subjects No. 26. HMSO, London. 1983

19. Department of Health and Social Security *Guidelines for the Testing of Chemicals for Mutagenicity* Reports on Health and Social Subjects No. 25. HMSO, London. 1983

20. Department of Health and Social Security *Guidance on the Preparation of Summaries of Data on Chemicals in Food, Consumer Products and the Environment Submitted to DHSS* Report on Health and Social Subjects No. 30. HMSO, London. 1986

21. Department of Health and Social Security *Diet and Cardiovascular Disease. Report of the Panel on Diet in Relation to Cardiovascular Disease. Committee on Medical Aspects of Food Policy* Report on Health and Social Subjects No. 28. HMSO, London. 1984

22. As Reference 16

23. Department of Health and Social Security *Nutritional Aspects of Bread and Flour: Report of the Panel on Bread, Flour and other Cereal Products. Committee on Medical Aspects of Food Policy.* Report on Health and Social Subjects. No. 23. HMSO, London. 1981

24. Fenner, Peggy (Parliamentary Secretary, Ministry of Agriculture, Fisheries and Food). Oral answer to Simon Coombs. Question on *Food Labelling Hansard* 6th Series Vol 101 col 433. 10 July 1986

25. Anonymous. COMA faces sugar mountain *Chemistry and Industry* 16 February 1987
26. Glinsman, W. H., Irauquin, H. and Park, Y. K. *Report from FDA's Sugars Task Force: Evaluation of Health Aspects of Sugars Contained in Carbohydrate Sweeteners.* Reprinted from *Journal of Nutrition* **116** No 11S November 1986
27. Department of Health and Social Security *Advisory Committee on Irradiated and Novel Foods. Report on the Safety and Wholesomeness of Irradiated Foods.* HMSO, London. 1986
28. As Reference 16
29. Ministry of Agriculture, Fisheries and Food *Consultative Document: Pesticides, Implementing Part III of the Food and Environment Protection Act, 1985.* Pesticides and Infestation Control Division, MAFF. November 1985
30. *Food and Environment Protection Act, 1985* Eliz 2 (1985 ch 48). HMSO, London. 1985
31. Ministry of Agriculture, Fisheries and Food *Food Advisory Committee Review of Additives to Cloud Soft Drinks* FAC/REP/2. Standards Division, MAFF, London. 1985. (for example)

The European connection

Since 1973, when the UK joined the European Economic Community (EEC)*, there has been a need to consider food legislation in a European context as well as the national context. Accession to the EEC has meant that several of the more recent instances of secondary legislation have been derived from European initiatives rather than domestic initiatives; in these circumstances, the principal administrative centre is Brussels rather than Whitehall, with British interests having a considerably smaller impact than would be the case with purely national legislation.

The impact of EEC considerations exists in two major forms:

1. Certain aspects of specific European food legislation have been incorporated into British legislation;
2. When preparing any national food legislation there is a necessity to examine how this fits within EEC legislation.

Main function of the EEC

In order to discuss the points listed above, it is worth examining briefly the main function of the EEC. This is set out in Article 2 of the 1957 *Treaty of Rome*[1], which established the Community:

> The Community shall have as its task, by establishing a common market and progressively approximating the economic policies of Member States to promote throughout the Community a harmonious development of economic activities, a continuous and balanced expansion, an increase in stability, an accelerated raising of the standard of living and closer relations between the States belonging to it.

* A brief introduction to the EEC and its institutions is given as *Appendix 2*

The key words are 'common market'. The common market provides for the free movement of goods and services between Member States. The movement of goods and services serves to create a single 'internal market' for the community as a whole, thereby superseding the concept of national markets within each Member State. Achievement of a single internal market requires the existence of a common set of controls which apply equally in all Member States.

The basic objectives are set out in the *Treaty of Rome* and the subsequent amending treaties. In many ways the Treaty may be regarded as *the* primary legislation of the EEC, with all other EEC legislation providing the detailed information in much the same manner that the *Food Act, 1984*[2] covers the generalities of British food law while Statutory Instruments made under it provide the details. The difference between the *Treaty of Rome* and the *Food Act* is, however, one of scope. Not only does the Treaty apply in all EEC Member States, it applies to a very wide range of community activities; food-related legislation is just one area.

Article 30 of the Treaty of Rome states that

> Quantitative restrictions on imports and all measures having equivalent effect shall . . . be prohibited between Member States.

This means that Member States must permit the free passage of legally produced goods (including foods) from one Member State to another. There are certain exceptions to this general rule, which are listed in *Article 36*. The only exception of direct relevance to foodstuffs relates to

> . . . the protection of health and life of humans, animals or plants . . .

Even under these exceptions

> prohibitions or restrictions shall not, however, constitute a means of arbitrary discrimination or a disguised restriction on trade between Member States.

This means that any exception on the grounds of a threat to public health will require strong and clear supporting evidence.

Harmonization

In addition to the above, the Treaty of Rome also includes provisions in Article 100 which permit the Council:

> to issue directives for the approximation of such provisions laid down by law, regulation or administrative action in Member States as directly affect the establishment or functioning of the Common Market.

In essence, this means that the EEC may lay down standards which apply throughout the Community. These standards may relate to food-stuffs. This process of approximation of laws is also referred to as harmonization. The present position with regard to harmonization is summarized in *Table 7.1*.

Horizontal and vertical measures

As with Britain's national food regulations, EEC standards may be divided into two major groups:

1. Those which apply across a wide variety of foodstuffs. Controls on labelling, additives and other matters are commonly referred to as horizontal measures;
2. Those which apply solely to a specified foodstuff or closely defined group of foods. Rules which apply solely to sugar or to fruit juices (for example) are commonly referred to as vertical measures.

Table 7.1   EEC harmonization

Stage reached	Subject
Subjects covered by Directives	1. Labelling of foodstuffs in general 2. Colouring agents 3. Preservatives 4. Antioxidants 5. Emulsifiers, stabilizers, thickeners and gelling agents 6. Materials and articles in contact with food (framework directive + several specific directives) 7. Foods for particular nutritional uses (framework directive) 8. Cocoa and chocolate 9. Sugar 10. Honey 11. Fruit juices and similar products 12. Jams, jellies and marmalades 13. Preserved milk 14. Caseins and caseinates 15. Coffee and chicory extracts 16. Natural mineral waters
Subjects before the Council of Ministers	1. Amendments to labelling, foods for particular nutritional uses, additives generally, materials and articles in contact with food 2. Flavourings 3. Extraction solvents 4. Chemically modified starches 5. Frozen foods 6. Infant formulae and follow-up milks
Subjects for which Directives are in preparation within the Commission	1. New categories of additives 2. Irradiation 3. Inspection measures

As can be noted from *Table 7.1*, progress on vertical measures has been relatively slow, with compositional and other standards having been reached for only a very small number of food commodities. By contrast, United Kingdom measures apply to around 30 different commodity groups. However, several horizontal measures have been successfully introduced, particularly with regard to food additives, although here, too, the EEC has not fully achieved its initial objectives. Although common permitted lists for several classes of additive have been agreed, there has been no progress towards a harmonization of conditions of use. This means that each Member State may establish national controls which limit the use of particular additives, even to the extent of permitting use in only a single food. Member States continue to maintain national rules on the grounds that public health requirements differ from country to country. This view has been challenged on a number of occasions in the European Court. Two key test cases are the 'Nisin' case of 1980 and the 'Motte' case of 1985.

Nisin case

The Dutch authorities brought proceedings against a Dutch manufacturer of processed cheese on the grounds that the cheese contained an additive, nisin, which was not authorized for use in cheese under Dutch law. (Nisin is an antibiotic which occurs naturally in most types of cheese and which retards deterioration.) The manufacturer claimed in his defence that the amount of nisin added was not sufficient to present any hazard to health and that since the addition of nisin to cheese is permitted in other EEC Member States any prohibition would constitute a breach of the rules of the *Treaty of Rome* by acting as a 'measure having an effect equivalent to a quantitative restriction within the meaning of Articles 30 to 36 of the Treaty'. The Dutch authorities referred the case on appeal to the European Court, which pointed out the fact that differences in national laws do act as barriers to trade but in this case the Dutch reasons for prohibiting nisin were in accord with Article 36 — that is the 'the protection of health and life of humans'. The Court ruled as follows:

> . . . the provisions of the EEC Treaty regarding the free movement of goods do not, at the present stage of Community rules on preservatives in foodstuffs intended for human consumption, preclude national measures by a Member State which on the ground of the protection of health and in accordance with Article 36 of the Treaty, prohibit the addition of nisin to home-produced or imported processed cheese, even if they limit such a prohibition only to products intended for sale on the domestic market of that State.[3]

Motte case

This case was referred to the European Court by the Belgian Court of Appeal seeking interpretation of Article 36 of the *Treaty of Rome*. The Belgian authorities had brought proceedings against Leon Motte for importing into Belgium canned black and red lump-fish eggs which had been coloured with indigotin and cochineal A red respectively. The use of these colours in canned fish eggs was not permitted in Belgium although the colours were legally used in the country of origin, Germany. The colours were permitted in other foods sold in Belgium. This raised the question of whether the Belgian prohibition constituted a restriction in trade between Member States.

The Court noted that the Community legislation with respect to additives was only partially harmonized and that 'it is for Member States to decide the level of protection they wish to ensure for the health and life of persons'.

The Court concluded that Member States may apply limitations on the use of colours, thereby restricting access for products containing these colours, which are lawfully marketed in the exporting state. However, Community law does apply certain limitations to such restrictions.

> National authorities must authorise the colouring of the foodstuff if, having regard to the eating habits prevailing in the importing Member State, it corresponds to a real need, and in their appraisal of the general health risk which the colouring matter actually used may represent, those authorities must take into account the results of international scientific research and in particular the work of the Community's Scientific Committee for Food.[4]

Simplification of procedures

It is now agreed that Member States appear to be able to agree on general principles, but have difficulty achieving agreement on points of detail and, in particular, are unable to agree requirements for the composition of individual foodstuffs. This fact has been identified by the EEC Commission as a barrier to the completion of the internal market, and in view of this recognition, proposals have been published which seek to simplify procedures and thus avoid much of the necessity of confining 'in a legislative straitjacket the culinary riches of ten (twelve) European countries'. The Commission instead favours

> the fundamental idea that, provided that the purchaser is given adequate information on the nature and composition of foodstuffs, it is not necessary to define these elements in law unless they are required for the protection of public health.[5]

A shift towards the adoption of this principle is under way and a number of documents listing proposals have already been published.

The Commission proposals, which form a part of the Cockfield Initiative[6] (named after the EEC Commissioner responsible for the Internal Market) will be returned to later in this chapter. However, it is necessary to first of all consider briefly the sequence of events which currently take place during negotiations leading to the approximation of food laws.

Procedures preceding food legislation

As in Britain, the procedures are complex and involve numerous stages of documentation and consultation.

Proposals for any EEC measures are developed within the appropriate Directorate General of the EEC Commission. As in Britain, and elsewhere, the initial decision to consider an issue will arise for a variety of reasons as officials become aware that there is a 'need' for controls to be considered and subsequently established. However, it can be noted that whereas national controls seek to protect consumers' and traders' interests with respect to fair trading, and aim to provide safe food, the chief goal of the EEC measures is that of a single common set of rules to permit the development of a single internal market.

For many issues, when drawing up controls the EEC will seek expert advice from bodies specifically constituted for this purpose. The principal advisory bodies with regard to food legislation are:

1. Scientific Committee for Foods;
2. Advisory Committee on Foodstuffs;
3. Standing Committee for Foodstuffs.

These Committees have no direct parallels within Britain's national advisory bodies although, in principle, their purpose is broadly the same as that applying to the Committee on Toxicology of Chemicals in Food, Consumer Products and the Environment, the Committee on Medical Aspects of Food Policy and the Food Advisory Committee. They exist to provide advice and recommendations to those responsible for decisions relating to food quality and safety. In practice, however, the EEC Committees are constituted in a very different manner to those advising the UK government.

Scientific Committee for Foods

The EEC officials and legislators are advised on scientific and technical aspects by the Scientific Committee for Foods, which was established in 1974 as a permanent body which would act as a consultative committee. It is composed of not more than 15 members, each of whom is a 'highly qualified scientific person'. The Committee's deliberations relate only to 'opinions' requested by the EEC Commission. 'Opinions' may be requested on:

> any problem relating to the protection of the health and safety of persons arising from the consumption of food, and in particular on the composition of food, processes which are liable to modify food, the use of food additives and other processing aids as well as the presence of contaminants.[7]

Opinions of the Committee are submitted to the EEC Commission and are usually published in a series entitled *Reports of the Scientific Com-*

mittee for Food[8], one issue of which may contain 'opinions' on a number of topics.

As its title suggests, the Committee concentrates its attention on the scientific aspects of an issue and, in this respect, parallels the work undertaken in the UK by the Committee on Toxicity of Chemicals in Food, Consumer Products and the Environment (COT). However, the Committee does not possess the independence enjoyed by the COT because many members are officials, rather than independent scientists with no other involvement in the legislative process.

The Scientific Committee for Foods (like the COT) does not comment on the wider issues (such as 'need' for an additive) but leaves such aspects to others. During 1986, the House of Lords Select Committee on the European Communities recommended[9] that the Scientific Committee for Foods should be expanded to include a wider range of experts or, alternatively, an additional committee of independent experts be established to consider issues such as the 'need' for food additives.

Advisory Committee on Foodstuffs

The second body of relevance here is the Advisory Committee on Foodstuffs, which was established in 1975 with revised responsibilities from 1980[10]. The committee comprises permanent members together with experts appointed to assist them. Committee members are drawn from five economic groupings: agriculture, commerce, consumers, industry and employees. The Committee may be consulted by the Commission on 'all problems concerning the harmonization of legislation relating to foodstuffs'.

In general, the role of this Committee is to provide 'opinions' and versions of measures which the EEC Commission is already proposing. This feature is significantly different from the purely advisory role given to (for example) the Food Advisory Committee, which makes recommendations that may, at a later date, result in official proposals for action. The Committee does not take a vote on its opinions but, rather, evolves a consensus view by discussion of the matter in question.

Standing Committee on Foodstuffs

The third body of importance with regard to food legislation within the EEC system is the Standing Committee on Foodstuffs. This body was established in 1969[11] as a permanent Commission committee made up of government experts from Member States under the chairmanship of a Commission official. As with the Advisory Committee on Foodstuffs, the Standing Committee provides opinions on matters under consideration by the Commission. The Committee reaches its opinions by means of a majority vote — although current EEC Commission proposals[12], if implemented, would demote the status of the Committee and would remove the voting powers. Where the Committee agrees with the EEC Commission proposals, the Commission is bound to act on them. Where the Committee disagrees with the EEC Commission proposals, the Commission must immediately pass the matter to the EEC Council for decision; time limits are set for a decision to be reached and action taken. This procedure is outlined in each new directive at the proposal (COM doc) stage and is regarded as a significant consumer protection feature, which also serves to protect national interests.

Further steps in processing legislative proposals

Once a decision has been taken within the EEC Commission to consider a matter for statutory control, the system used to process legislative proposals relating to foods is identical to that applying to all other issues.

Directives

The system used by the EEC for considerations leading to legislation in general is summarized in *Figure 7.1*. In the case of food legislation, the controls have been given as 'Directives', which require national governments to take steps to implement them before they can have force of law. To ensure Member States comply with directives, dates are prescribed which state the latest date by which national legislation should be enacted. In Britain, food law directives are implemented by means of a statutory instrument, as discussed earlier. Examples of EEC Directives subsequently incorporated into British food legislation include the following relating to sugars:

1. EEC Directive: 1973/437[13]   General aspects relating to sugars; incorporated into British legislation by SI 1976 No 509;[14]
2. EEC Directive: 1979/796[15]   Purity criteria for sugars; incorporated into British legislation by SI 1982 No 255.[16]

Section 119 of the *Food Act, 1984* provides Ministers with the power to make regulations for the purpose of ensuring that Community provisions are administered, executed and enforced. When the UK joined the EEC, the decision was taken to use the basic food legislation (at that time the *Food and Drugs Act, 1955*[17]) to implement new food directives. (Directives which were already in force were included in the Treaty of Accession.) The *European Communities Act, 1972*[18] made a number of amendments to the 1955 Act to enable Ministers to make regulations 'called for by any Community obligation' in addition to existing powers relating to public health or the protection of the public.

Regulations

As shown in *Figure 7.1*, there is a second category of EEC controls, known as Regulations. For certain foodstuffs EEC legislation has been applied as part of agricultural policy rather than policy relating to the internal market. (A key food in this respect is milk which, as in UK legislation, is treated in some ways as a special case.) Where legislation relates to agricultural policy it has been customary to make regulations

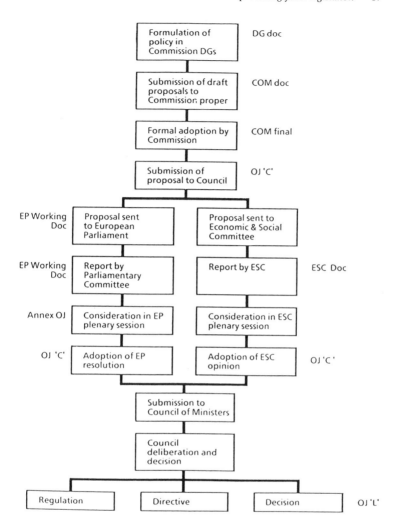

Figure 7.1 Summary of the legislative process in the European Communities. The abbreviations, which primarily are used to indicate publication details of EEC documents (given alongside the flow chart), are as follows: DG, Directorate General (equivalent to a Ministry within a national government), e.g. DG VI deals with agriculture and DG III deals with the internal market; EP, European Parliament (*Appendix 2* gives an introduction to the various EEC institutions including the European Parliament and Economic and Social Committee); ESC, Economic and Social Committee; COM doc, Document submitted by EEC officials to the European Community; COM final, Document agreed as proposed from the European Commission to the Council; OJ, Official Journal of the European Communities; OJ 'C', as above (volume dealing with notices and information); OJ 'L', as above (volume dealing with legislation). It should be noted that the Council deliberations themselves involve several stages, including the consideration of specific aspects by working groups

under Article 43 of the *Treaty of Rome*. EEC Regulations do not require national action but are directly applicable to all Member States, although in certain circumstances it may be necessary to use national legislation to clarify aspects of an EEC regulation in order to facilitate compliance or enforcement.

With regard to food legislation the use of EEC Regulations is rare (Directives are much more usual). A notable exception is EEC Regulation 1411 of 1971[19], which limited the specifications of liquid milks sold within the Community to the following:

1. Raw milk — (i.e. not heat treated);
2. Standardized heat-treated milk of not less than 3.5% butterfat;
3. Half-skimmed heat-treated milk with butterfat content of 1.5–1.8%;
4. Skimmed heat-treated milk with maximum butterfat content of 0.3%

This regulation, agreed before the UK joined the EEC, excludes the type of milk most commonly consumed in the UK — non-standardized heat-treated milk — and it was necessary to agree an amendment (EEC Regulation 566 of 1976[20]) to permit the continued sale of this item once the UK fully adopted the EEC rules following a transition period.

Consultation system

The summary in *Figure 7.1* shows also that, as with British legislation, there is considerable opportunity for contributions to be made to the decision-making procedures. However, because the legislation is to be supranational, the main direct contributors are national government officials and the international trade and consumer associations. Within Britain, wide comment is specifically invited on draft Directives and usually the UK position in negotiations is decided in close consultation with interested parties in industry, retailing, consumer organizations and enforcement authorities.

As with national legislation, these consultations are confined essentially to those organizations on the Ministry's mailing list as the consultations do not receive general publicity. The EEC system of consultation has been criticized from within the Commission itself on the grounds that there is disproportionately little input from consumer interests. In its paper on the *New Impetus for Consumer Protection* published in 1985 the Directorate General for Consumer Services said:

> Community efforts to increase awareness of consumer protection issues depend for their success not only on the pursuit of specific actions, but also upon the extent to which consumer interests are taken into account when formulating and executing other Community policies. To ensure the necessary degree of interpenetration of consumer protection and other policies, consumer representatives must be consulted on Community measures that significantly affect their interests. Only in this way can their viewpoint be taken adequately into account.[21]

As will be noted in detail later, this message does not appear to have influenced the thinking of those wishing to streamline decision making with respect to the Community's Internal Market.

Because any Directive is at least nominally considered by the European Parliament, there exists opportunity for intervention by Members of the European Parliament. However, in view of the very wide variety of topics considered by the European Parliament, debate is very unlikely.

The sequence of events listed in *Figure 7.1* results in a number of documents being made available at the various stages. However, it is fair to say that these papers are not generally available except in those libraries which particularly serve as European Documentation Centres.

Timescale

The EEC sequence of events described above and in *Figure 7.1* has elements of both Parliamentary and Official consideration. However, the relative remoteness and complexity of EEC procedures generally lead to a very slow consideration of the issues. This is because there is a need for each member state to ascertain the views of interested parties within its boundaries before entering each stage of the deliberations. For example, the British regulations currently in force with respect to jams etc. derive from an EEC Directive published in the *Official Journal* in July 1979; this Directive in turn was based on an amended Commission Proposal published in the *Official Journal* in September 1975 and considered by the European Parliament and by the Economic and Social Committee during 1976; the amended proposals were themselves based on originals prepared during the mid-1960s. The final Jams Directive was based, to a great extent, on the international standard elaborated by the Codex Alimentarius Commission (see Chapter 8). The additional discussions in an international forum undoubtedly helped to resolve some of the basic differences between Member States of the EEC.

Removal of trade barriers

The complexity of procedures towards approximation of laws relating to foods has contributed to a situation in which harmonization is less favoured than was the case in the past. Nowadays, barriers to trade are likely to be removed by actions which will permit any product legally manufactured and sold in one member state to be legally sold in any other.

This principle has been established in the European Court in a case generally referred to as the Cassis de Dijon Case.

German food laws: Cassis de Dijon case

Cassis de Dijon is a blackcurrant liquor with alcohol content of between 15% and 20%. The product is manufactured and freely marketed in France but when, in 1976, German importers attempted to sell the liquor in Germany, they came into conflict with German legislation which required fruit liquors to have a minimum alcohol content of 25%. When prevented from selling Cassis de Dijon, the would-be importers appealed to the European Court, claiming that the provisions in German law prevent well-known products from other Member States being sold in Germany and thus was equivalent to a quantitative restriction on imports and contrary to Article 30 of the *Treaty of Rome*. In reaching its decision the Court commented that

> Obstacles to movement within the Community resulting from disparities between the national laws relating to the marketing of products in question must be accepted insofar as those provisions may be recognised as being necessary in order to satisfy mandatory requirements relating in particular to the effectiveness of fiscal supervision, the protection of public health, the fairness of commercial transactions and the defence of the consumer.[22]

However, the Court ruled that the requirements stipulated by the German authorities did not comply with these criteria. The Cassis de Dijon judgement is often paraphrased and oversimplified to read:

> if a product is legally manufactured and marketed in one Member State then it may also be legally sold in any other member state.

However, it is necessary to remember the conditions stated by the Court.

The irony of the judgement is that importers may now legally sell a product such as Cassis de Dijon throughout the Community, but a German manufacturer cannot sell such a product on his home market because he remains subject to the original German law.

German food laws: beer

The German food laws have also been disputed by other EEC members with regard to beer. The 'Reinheitsgebot' (Pledge of Purity) of 1516 limits German brewers to the ingredients barley, hops, yeast and water. Much of the beer brewed in other EEC countries includes other ingredients and has been excluded from the German market. The European Court finally ruled on the Reinheitsgebot in March 1987[23] and the EEC now requires Germany to allow access to the German market for beer from other Member States, provided that this complies with the legislation in the country of origin. As with the Cassis de Dijon case, the German brewer must still comply with the long-established national law.

There are clear exceptions to the generalization that a Member State may not make compositional or labelling regulations which act as non-tariff barriers to trade. For instance, measures may be taken to prevent fraud or unfair competition, or a case may be made that such a requirement is necessary for the protection of public health, in which case the conditions given in *Article 30* of the *Treaty of Rome* are overriden by those in *Article 36*. This last argument is central to current UK proposals for the labelling of foodstuffs with an indication of their fat content[24], which form part of the government's response to the

Report of the COMA Panel on Diet in Relation to Cardiovascular Disease[25]. It remains to be seen whether the EEC will accept the argument that such labelling is necessary on public health grounds. The UK government is arguing that, as cardiovascular disease death rates are particularly high in the UK, this measure is necessary for the protection of public health.

EEC overruling of UK measures

The United Kingdom has previously had national measures overruled by EEC considerations relating to the single internal market.

Until 1983, the UK liquid milk market was totally protected from imports. Historically, imports were prevented by practical and economic constraints but, more recently, conditions laid down in the regulations which controlled the hygienic quality of milk acted as a non-tariff barrier. The regulations[26] stipulated that milk should be bottled or packed only on premises registered with the local authority in whose area they were located. This condition excluded foreign milk from the UK market, because no local authority could license any packer located outside its boundary.

In February 1983, the European Court ruled[27] that this regulation was being used simply as an excuse to protect the UK industry from competition, and hence was in breach of the basic provisions of the Treaty of Rome. The Court upheld the right of the UK to ensure that imported foods (including milk) present no hazard to human or animal health but judged that the method used in this instance was excessive. The case related specifically to ultra-heat-treated (UHT) milk.

During 1983, MAFF drew up new legislation to control quality of imports[28]. Detailed regulations[29] were laid before Parliament on 26 October 1983, and a negative resolution debate was initiated by the Opposition on 16 November 1983[30]. The debate was heated, but the new regulations were approved. Milk imports began early in December 1983, but imports have not taken a significant proportion of the market, achieving only 0.03% of total milk sales. To date, imports have been restricted to UHT and sterilized milks, both of which are relatively small markets when compared with the market for pasteurized.

It is inevitable that the UK market will, in due course, be open to imports of pasteurized milk. The EEC has initiated proceedings similar to the earlier one which related only to UHT. However, it seems likely that the major shift will follow the application of EEC *Directive 85/397*[31] which relates to the 'health and animal health problems affecting intra-Community trade in heat treated milk'. In essence, this directive seeks to standardize health standards applying to milk throughout the EEC, thereby removing a potential barrier to trade. Throughout the discussions leading to *Directive 85/397*, the UK Government stressed that any reduction in the standards currently applying in the UK would be unacceptable, the harmonization of standards being possible only at the high standards already reached by the UK.

Transition to such a standard will require significant changes in some Member States, and a two-stage implementation is envisaged. Stage 1 will be achieved by all Member States by the date at which the directive comes into effect (1 January 1989). Stage 2 will be more stringent and will be progressively implemented in subsequent years. The date, 1 April 1990, has been proposed with reference to milk for direct human consumption. The second stage will be extended to all milk at a later date: 1 January 1993 has been proposed, although the directive does allow for postponement to 1995 if necessary.

States such as the UK, which already meet the Stage 2 standards, will be able to apply such standards to imports without a transition period. Once the directive comes into force (1 January 1989), exporting governments will be required to certify that milk complies with the required standards and importing states will have the power to check imports before sale. The ability to block imports from other EEC Member States will be lost.

From the above examples, it may be noted that the principal condition imposed on national legislation is that legal measures must not go further than is genuinely necessary to achieve the desired objective. The term used to describe this degree of control is 'proportionate to their purpose'. In the UHT milk example, the European Court ruled that the restrictions were disproportionate and could be removed without causing problems for animal health in Britain.

Progress towards unification of food legislation

The principle of 'proportionate to their purpose' has also been accepted with regard to EEC-wide measures, and is a major theme in the Commission White Paper published in November 1985 entitled *Completion of the Internal Market: Community Legislation on Foodstuffs*[32]. This paper reviewed progress towards a unified system of food legislation and is worthy of close examination because it re-evaluates a number of the principal features of the EEC harmonization process.

The paper arose from a recognition by the EEC Commission that a genuine common market could not be achieved in the near future without a shift away from the traditional methods of harmonization. Harmonization was initially conceived because it was accepted that barriers to trade could be overcome only through the establishment of community-wide standards. The harmonization programme was initiated in 1969 with this objective, but progress has generally been slow.

In addition, there has had to be a rethink of methods subsequent to the EEC Court of Justice ruling on Cassis de Dijon, referred to earlier. The acceptance of the principle that a product lawfully manufactured and marketed in one Member State may also be marketed in all other Member States means that requirements stipulated in national legislation do not necessarily act as a barrier to trade.

In recognition of both these points, the EEC Commission is now proposing that:

future legislation be limited to provisions justified by the need to

1. protect public health
2. provide customers with information and protection in matters

   other than health
3. ensure fair trading
4. provide for the necessary public controls.

Matters requiring legislation

In respect of the above, the Commission identified the matters noted below as those requiring legislation.

Public health generally

All Member States have national legislation relating to public health and although each State's rules are based on the same basic objective, there are frequent instances where national rules act as a barrier to trade. Harmonization (such as described earlier with regard to liquid milk) would remove the necessity for mutual recognition of public health standards.

Food additives

The EEC has established positive lists for several categories of food additive, and it is accepted that there would be benefit in drawing up positive lists for those categories not yet dealt with.

Materials in contact with foodstuffs

Community measures already exist with regard to this topic, and it is recognized that continued EEC legislation is desirable.

Foods for particular dietetic uses

Again, general principles have been accepted for some time, and the chief requirement is for further clarification.

Processes for the manufacture or treatment of foods

Specific controls are rarely required with respect to processes. EEC proposals exist with regard to deep freezing and are planned with respect to irradiation and biotechnology.

   Each of the above topics is justified with regard to the need to protect public health. Other matters which the EEC Commission consider to require legislation are as follows.

Consumer information and protection (matters other than health)

The bulk of compositional and labelling standards exist for reasons of consumer protection rather than for reasons of health promotion. Composition Standards — otherwise known as recipe law — are progressively becoming outmoded as manufacturers can develop food products at a rate which precludes legislative control, while legislative rigidity would result in an unnecessary 'obstacle to innovation and commercial flexibility'. The EEC Commission now accepts that if the consumer is provided with adequate information on the nature and composition of a food, then 'recipe law' is unnecessary.

Labelling

From the above, it follows that labelling should continue as a matter requiring legislative controls. The EEC Commission favours a tightening of controls to eliminate derogations at national level with respect to (for example) ways of specifying additives in the list of ingredients. In addition, the EEC Commission is consulting Member States with regard to labelling with nutrition information.

Fair trading

Principles relating to fair trading are accepted and will continue to be reflected in legislation.

Proposals

Subsequent to the initial paper on the *Completion of the Internal Market: Community Legislation on Foodstuffs*, the Commission has released proposals on five topics:

1. Additives[33]
2. Labelling[34]
3. Material in contact with foodstuffs[35]
4. Foods for specific nutritional uses[36]
5. Official inspection of foodstuffs[37]

At the time of writing (at the beginning of 1988), these are in the form of draft directives, copies of which have been circulated to interested parties by the Ministry of Agriculture, Fisheries and Food, and published in the *Official Journal of the European Communities*. In addition, the Commission has prepared a timetable listing a series of proposals which it plans to release in the years to 1990 in order to meet its objective of completing the Internal Market by the year 1992.

Reservations and criticisms

Most people agree that progress towards harmonization has been excessively slow and that the proposals for change in the structure of the EEC legislation offer opportunities for the achievement of the goal of a common internal market. However, there are fears that the simplified structure will not offer the degree of either consumer protection or protection of national interests to be found in present procedures. The Standards Division of the Ministry of Agriculture, Fisheries and Food believe that

> the procedural provisions of the draft directive, as they stand, are clearly designed to strengthen the Commission's competence in this area . . . thereby weakening the influence of Member States.[38]

These views have been reiterated and expanded in a paper from the Consumers in the European Community Group[39] which makes detailed criticism of the proposals and comments that the White Paper, with its emphasis on speeding up the removal of barriers to trade does not offer enough protection of consumer's safety and economic interests.

In addition to the White Paper on the internal market for foodstuffs, the Community has also amended its decision-making systems significantly through the adoption of the *Single European Act*[40] (see *Appendix 2*) which introduced majority voting into many aspects of community policy including the legislation relating to foodstuffs. This has significant implications for the UK food manufacturing industry and consumers because, even if UK legislators are convinced of the need for a particular course of action, it is possible that they may be outvoted by representatives from other Member States.

Returning to the White Paper, a number of key points can be noted as worthy of particular comment as they serve to modify substantially long-accepted decision-making processes. For example, the White Paper refers to a framework directive for food additives (since published as a proposal) which would set out the basic criteria for approval of additives which have been evaluated by the Scientific Committee for Food. However, the paper goes on to state:

> Once these various requirements have been met, the task of drawing up the approved list and relevant conditions of use may be given to the Commission.

This represents a major shift from the view set out in the Motte case described earlier, in which national governments set limits after taking full acount of national dietary habits. The procedures described in Chapter 6 (in which the Committee on Toxicity of Chemicals in Food Consumer Products and the Environment assesses safety aspects of additives while a separate body, the Food Advisory Committee, assesses need and makes recommendations for conditions of use in foods sold in the United Kingdom) offer a substantially more rigorous system of consumer protection than do the simplified procedures now proposed for the EEC as a whole.

A second criticism which has been raised is the demotion of the role of the Standing Committee on Foodstuffs. At present the Committee will vote on proposed legislation and there are defined procedures to be followed subsequent to the vote. (These procedures are set out in the Memorandum which accompanies the Draft Directive from the Commission to Member States). In the Proposed Framework Directives issued subsequent to the White Paper, the Standing Committee on Foodstuffs is reduced to an advisory role without the opportunity for a vote to be taken.

The above two examples serve to illustrate the manner in which the EEC food legislative system is shifting in order to achieve a single 'common market'. As was pointed out in the opening paragraph of the chapter, EEC considerations are nowadays central to any examination of the system of food legislation applying within the United Kingdom. The influence of the EEC is, perhaps, the major factor in shaping current food legislation.

References

1. *Treaty Establishing the European Economic Community* signed in Rome 25 March 1957. An abridged version of this Treaty is published in *Treaties Establishing the European Communities* Office for Official Publications of the European Communities, Luxembourg. 1983
2. *Food Act, 1984* Eliz 2 (1984 ch 30) HMSO, London. 1984
3. Officier van Justitie v Koninklijke Kaasfabriek Eyssen BV (preliminary ruling requested by the Gerechtshof, Amsterdam) *Free Movement of Goods — Prohibition of Additives* Judgement of the Court of Justice of the European Communities. Case 53/80. 5 February 1981. Reports of Cases Before the Court. Vol 2, pp 409–432. 1981
4. Ministere Public v Leon Motte (Reference for a Preliminary ruling) 10 December 1985 *Measures equivalent in effect to quantitative restrictions — Directive introducing partial harmonisation — Colorants. Proceedings of the Court of Justice of the European Communities* 26/85. Weeks of 2 to 5 December and 9 to 13 December 1985
5. Commission of the European Communities *Completion of the Internal Market: Community Legislation on Foodstuffs* Communication from the Commission to the Council and to the European Parliament. COM (85) 603 final. Office for Official Publications of the European Communities, Luxembourg. 1985
6. Commission of the European Communities *Completing the Internal Market.* White Paper from the Commission to the European Council (Milan, 28 and 29 June 1985) COM (85) 310 final. Office for Official Publications of the European Communities, Luxembourg. 1985
7. Commission of the European Communities *Commission Decision of 17 April 1974 relating to the institution of a Scientific Committee for Food* (74/234/EEC). *Official Journal of the European Communities* L 136/1. 20 May 1974
8. Commission of the European Communities. Directorate General — Internal Market and Industrial Affairs *Reports of the Scientific Committee for Food.* Office for Official Publications of the European Communities, Luxembourg. Irregular
9. *Internal Market for Foodstuffs 13th Report of the House of Lords Select Committee on the European Communities* HL (1985-86) 166. HMSO, London. 1986
10. Commission of the European Communities *Commission Decision of 24 October 1980 establishing new Statute of the Advisory Committee on Foodstuffs* (80/1073/EEC). *Official Journal of the European Communities* L 318/28. 26 November 1980
11. Council of the European Communities *Decision of the Council of 13 November 1969, instituting a Standing Committee for Foodstuffs* (69/414/EEC). *Official Journal of the European Communities* L 291/9. 19 November 1969
12. See for example: Article 9 of: Commission of the European Communities *Proposal for a Council Directive on the Approximation of the Member States Concerning Food Additives Authorised for Use in Foodstuffs Intended for Human Consumption* COM (86) 87 Final. *Official Journal of the European Communities* C 116/2. 16 May 1986
13. Council of the European Communities *Council Directive of 11 December 1973 on the approximation of the laws of the Member States concerning certain sugars intended for human consumption* 73/437/EEC. *Official Journal of the European Communities* L 356/71. 27 December 1973
14. *Specified Sugar Products Regulations, 1976* SI No 509. HMSO, London. 1976

15. Commission of the European Communities *First Commission Directive of 26 July 1979 Laying down Community methods of analysis for testing sugars intended for human consumption* 79/786/EEC. *Official Journal of the European Communities* L 239/24. 22 September 1979

16. *Specified Sugar Products (Amendment) Regulations, 1982* SI No 255. HMSO, London. 1982

17. *Food and Drugs Act, 1955* Eliz 2 (1955 ch 16) HMSO, London. 1955

18. *European Communities Act, 1972* Eliz 2 (1972 ch 8) HMSO, London. 1972

19. Council of the European Communities *Council Regulation (EEC) No 1411/71 of 29 June 1971 Establishing the Complementary Rules for the Organisation of the Common Market for the Milk Sector and for Milk Products as they Relate to Position 04.01 of the Common Customs Tariff* 1411/71/EEC. *Official Journal of the European Communities* L 148/4. 3 July 1971

20. Council of the European Communities *Council Regulation (EEC) No 566/76 amending Regulation (EEC) No 1411/71 as regards the fat content of the whole milk. Official Journal of the European Communities* L 67/23. 15 March 1976

21. Commission of the European Communities *A New Impetus for Consumer Protection* COM (85) 314 final (Communication from the Commission to the Council) Office for Official Publications of the European Communities, Luxembourg. 1985

22. Rewe-Zentral AG V Bundesmonopolverwaltung fur Branntwein (preliminary ruling requested by the Hessisches Finanzgericht) *Measures having an effect equivalent to quantitative restrictions.* Judgement of the Court of Justice of the European Communities. Case 120/78. 20 February 1979. *Reports of Cases Before the Court* Vol 2 1979, pp.649–675

23. Peel, Q. W. German beer law overruled. *Financial Times* 13 March 1987

24. First announced as follows: Michael Jopling (Minister for Agriculture, Fisheries and Food) in a reply to Sir Peter Mills' Question on *Food Labelling. Hansard* 6th Series, Vol 75, col. 79–81. 12 March 1985

25. Department of Health and Social Security *Diet and Cardiovascular Disease. Report of the Panel on Diet in Relation to Cardiovascular Disease. Committee on Medical Aspects of Food Policy*, Report on Health and Social Subjects No 28. HMSO, London. 1984

26. *Milk and Dairies (General Regulations, 1959)* SI No 277. HMSO, London. 1959

27. Commission of the European Communities v United Kingdom of Great Britain and Northern Ireland. *Failure of a Member State to fulfil its obligations — Measures having an effect equivalent to quantitative restrictions — Milk Sterilised by the UHT process.* Judgement of the Court of Justice of the European Communities. Case 124/81. 8 February 1983. *Reports of Cases Before the Court* Vol 2 1983, pp.203–253

28. *Importation of Milk Act, 1983* Eliz 2 (1983 ch 37). HMSO, London. 1983

29. A total of 11 statutory instruments were laid before Parliament on 26 October 1983 in order that the UK might comply with the Judgement of Case 124/81 (above). Principal amongst these instruments was: *Importation of Milk Regulations, 1983* SI No 1563. HMSO, London. 1983

30. Debate praying against the 11 statutory instruments introduced to comply with the Judgement of Case 124/81. *Hansard* 6th Series Vol 48, col 898–959. 16 November 1983

31. Council of the European Communities *Council Directive of 5 August 1985 on health and animal-health problems affecting intra-Community trade in heat-treated milk* 85/397/EEC. *Official Journal of the European Communities* L 226/13. 24 August 1985

32. COM (85) 603 final op.cit. (reference 5)

33. COM (86) 87 final op.cit. (reference 12)

34. Commission of the European Communities *Proposal for a Council Direct-*

ive amending Directive 79/112/EEC on the approximation of the laws of the Member States relating to the labelling, presentation and advertising of foodstuffs for sale to the ultimate consumer COM (86) 89 final. *Official Journal of the European Communities* C 124/06. 23 May 1986

35. Commission of the European Communities *Proposal for a Council Directive on the approximation of the laws of the Member States relating to materials and articles intended to come into contact with foodstuffs* COM (86) 90 final. *Official Journal of the European Communities* C 124/07. 23 May 1986

36. Commission of the European Communities *Proposal for a Council Directive on the approximation of the laws of the Member States relating to foodstuffs intended for particular nutritional uses* COM (86) 91. *Official Journal of the European Communities* C 124/06. 23 May 1986

37. Commission of the European Communities *Proposal for a Council Directive on the official inspection of foodstuffs* COM (86) 747 final. *Official Journal of the European Communities* C20/6. 27 January 1987

38. Letter from Standards Division of MAFF to Interested Parties 12 June 1986 (Sent with copy of COM (86) 87 Final op.cit. (reference 12))

39. *Comments by Consumers in the European Community Group on the Completion of the Internal Market: Community Legislation on Foodstuffs (COM (85) 603).* Consumers in the European Community Group, London. 1986

40. *Single European Act* signed at Luxembourg on 17 February 1986 and at The Hague, 28 February 1986. Published in Council of the European Communities *Single European Act and Final Act*, Office for Official Publications of the European Communities, Luxembourg. 1986

Codex Alimentarius

Control of food standards has a further international aspect through the work of the Codex Alimentarius Commission. The Commission was established in the early 1960s after international initiatives, which began when the 1961 FAO Conference accepted proposals for the initiation of a programme of activities designed to remove those non-tariff barriers to trade in foods that were caused by differences in national food standards legislation. A joint committee of government experts in food standards was established and a conference co-sponsored by the United Nations Food and Agriculture Organization (FAO) and the World Health Organization (WHO) took place in 1962.

Role of the Codex Alimentarius and Joint FAO/WHO Food Standards Programme

The conference endorsed a proposal for the establishment of a joint FAO/WHO Food Standards Programme. The role of the Codex Alimentarius Commission is to implement the Joint FAO/WHO Food Standards Programme, the purposes of which are as follows[1]:

To protect the health of consumers and to ensure fair practices in the food trade
To promote co-ordination of all food standards work undertaken by international governmental and non-governmental organisations
To determine priorities and initiate and guide the preparation of draft standards through and with the aid of appropriate organisations
To finalise standards and after acceptance by governments to publish them in a Codex Alimentarius either as regional or world-wide standards.

At the time of its 16th session held in July 1985, 129 countries (listed in *Table 8.1)* were members of the Commission[2]. Members of the Commission are governments which also belong to FAO and/or WHO. In order to become a Commission member it is necessary only that a

Table 8.1   List of Member Countries of the Codex Alimentarius Commission (as at 1 October 1985)

AFRICA

1. Algeria
2. Benin
3. Botswana
4. Burkina Faso
5. Burundi
6. Camaroon
7. Cape Verde
8. Central African Republic
9. Chad
10. Congo
11. Egypt
12. Ethiopia
13. Gabon
14. Gambia
15. Ghana
16. Guinea
17. Guinea-Bissau
18. Ivory Coast
19. Kenya
20. Lesotho
21. Liberia
22. Libya
23. Madagascar
24. Malawi
25. Mauritius
26. Morocco
27. Mozambique
28. Nigeria
29. Senegal
30. Seychelles
31. Sierra Leone
32. Sudan
33. Swaziland
34. Tanzania
35. Togo
36. Tunisia
37. Uganda
38. Zaire
39. Zambia
40. Zimbabwe

ASIA

41. Bahrain
42. Bangladesh
43. Burma
44. China, People's Republic of
45. Democratic Kampuchea
46. India
47. Indonesia
48. Iran
49. Iraq
50. Japan
51. Jordan
52. Korea, People's Dem. Rep. of

53. Korea, Republic of
54. Kuwait
55. Lebanon
56. Malaysia
57. Nepal
58. Oman, Sultanate of
59. Pakistan
60. Philippines
61. Qatar
62. Saudi Arabia
63. Singapore
64. Sri Lanka
65. Syria
66. Thailand
67. United Arab Emirates
68. Viet-Nam
69. Yemen, People's Dem. Rep. of.

EUROPE

70. Austria
71. Belgium
72. Bulgaria
73. Cyprus
74. Czechoslovakia
75. Denmark
76. Finland
77. France
78. Germany, Fed. Rep. of
79. Greece
80. Hungary
81. Iceland
82. Ireland
83. Israel
84. Italy
85. Luxembourg
86. Malta
87. Netherlands
88. Norway
89. Poland
90. Portugal
91. Romania
92. Spain
93. Sweden
94. Switzerland
95. Turkey
96. United Kingdom
97. USSR
98. Yugoslavia

LATIN AMERICA

99. Argentina
100. Barbados
101. Bolivia
102. Brazil
103. Chile
104. Colombia
105. Costa Rica
106. Cuba

107. Dominican Republic
108. Ecuador
109. El Salvador
110. Grenada
111. Guatemala
112. Guyana
113. Haiti
114. Jamaica
115. Mexico
116. Nicaragua
117. Panama
118. Paraguay
119. Peru
120. Suriname
121. Trinidad and Tobago
122. Uruguay
123. Venezuela

NORTH AMERICA

124. Canada
125. USA

SOUTH WEST PACIFIC

126. Australia
127. Fiji
128. New Zealand
129. Samoa

---

country notify the Director General of FAO or WHO of its desire for membership. Membership does not require any financial commitment by member states except where a country undertakes to complete a task on behalf of the Commission. Membership does, however, confer rights of participation and election in the Commission activities together with the right to receive Codex documents. It is through receipt of these papers that the greater part of international communication on matters relating to food standards takes place.

In addition to representatives of national governments, the Commission has granted observer status to a number of international bodies including, for example, the European Economic Community, the International Dairy Federation, and the International Organization of Consumers' Unions.

The Codex Alimentarius itself is principally a collection of internationally agreed commodity standards which are presented in a uniform format, using the following headings:

1. Name of the standard;
2. Scope;
3. Description;
4. Essential composition and quality factors;
5. Food additives;
6. Contaminants;

7. Hygiene;
8. Weights and measures;
9. Labelling;
10. Methods of analysis and sampling.

The Codex Alimentarius includes standards for all the principal foods, whether processed, semi-processed or raw. In addition to the formally accepted standards, the Codex Alimentarius also includes provisions which are advisory. These include Codes of Practice and Guidelines.
   In addition to the commodity standards, the Codex has also established general provisions relating to labelling, additives, pesticide residues, hygiene, methods of analysis.

The principal aim of the Food Standards Programme is to facilitate international trade in foodstuffs while ensuring for all consumers a 'sound, wholesome product free from adulteration, correctly labelled and presented'. These principles are essentially the same as those underlying (at a national level) the provisions set out in the *Food Act* and its subordinate legislation.

Procedure for production of Codex Standards

As with national standards, Codex Standards are produced by a formal procedure. The system is not unlike the public bill procedures in the Houses of Parliament, as it consists of a number of steps which involve working committees and discussions by the Commission itself. Governments are involved throughout by attendance of delegates and by making formal and detailed written comments, as outlined below.

Step 1

A decision is taken by the Codex Alimentarius Commission that a standard should be drawn up. Also decided at this stage is which 'subsidiary body' should undertake the work. Subsidiary bodies are usually Codex Committees chaired by a member country. Responsibilities and host governments include the following.

Codex Committees and Intergovernmental Groups of Experts Dealing with Food Commodities Codex Committees

1. Edible fats and oils (United Kingdom);
2. Processed fruits and vegetables (United States of America);
3. Cereals, pulses and legumes (United States of America);
4. Foods for special dietary uses (Federal Republic of Germany);
5. Processed meat and poultry products (Denmark);
6. Fish and fishery products (Norway);
7. Vegetable proteins (Canada);
8. Cocoa products and chocolate (Switzerland);

  9. Sugars (United Kingdom);
10. Edible ices (Sweden);
11. Soups and broths (Switzerland);
12. Meat (Federal Republic of Germany);
13. Meat hygiene (New Zealand);
14. Natural mineral waters (Switzerland).

Intergovernmental Groups of Experts

1. Quick frozen food (FAO/WHO and UNECE);
2. Fruit juices (FAO/WHO and UNECE);
3. Milk and milk products (FAO/WHO).

Codex Committees Dealing with Subject Matters

Committees on the following topics may be substituted for the two groups of experts listed in the preceding sections:

1. Pesticide residues (Netherlands);
2. Food additives (Netherlands);
3. Methods of analysis and sampling (Hungary);
4. General principles (France);
5. Food labelling (Canada);
6. Food hygiene (United States of America);
7. Residues of veterinary drugs in foods (United States of America).

Codex Committees Dealing with Regional Matters

Alternatively, the following Regional Committees may be set up:

1. Regional Codex Coordinating Committee for Africa;
2. Regional Codex Coordinating Committee for Asia;
3. Regional Codex Coordinating Committee for Europe;
4. Regional Codex Coordinating Committee for Latin America and the Caribbean.

In addition, the subsidiary bodies receive advice from other international advisory bodies such as the Joint FAO/WHO Expert Committee on Food Additives (JECFA) or the Joint FAO/WHO Meeting on Pesticide Residues.

Bodies such as JECFA comprise individual experts who have specialized knowledge and experience. The members serve in an individual personal capacity and make recommendations based on specific and technical considerations.

Step 2

A 'proposed draft standard' is prepared by the Codex Committee with the assistance of the Secretariat of the Joint Programme.

Step 3

The first draft of the standard is sent to governments and to interested international organizations for comment. This includes comments on possible implications for their economic interests.

As part of their deliberations, Codex commodity committees will seek advice and guidance from the general subject committees with regard to points coming within their province (for example, with regard to food additives or labelling) and the relevant provisions in the standard have to be endorsed by these general committees.

Step 4

The text of the proposed standard is then considered again by the Codex Committee with regard to comments received.

Step 5

The proposed draft standard is submitted to the Commission for adoption as a 'draft standard'. Decisions taken at this stage take account of any comments received from governments.

Steps 6 and 7

Comments are again requested, received by the Secretariat and passed to the Codex Committee.

Step 8

The text is considered again by the Codex Committee in the light of discussions in the Commission and of government written comments. The Codex Committee draws up a final text and submits it to the Commission for consideration and approval as a 'Codex Standard'.

Codex Standard distribution

The Codex Standard is then published and sent to governments for acceptance, in accordance with the rules which have been carefully drawn up to take account of the need to ensure that a product which conforms to a Codex Standard will be freely distributed, whereas one which does not, will not be sold under the same description. Governments may specify certain deviations from the Codex Standard which must be complied with. If governments cannot accept the standard, they are asked to state whether a conforming product may be freely distributed, if necessary with conditions. Acceptance will usually involve new legislation or amendments to existing laws or regulations.

A full list of Codex final texts is available from the Codex Alimentarius Commission in Rome.

Code of Ethics

In addition to the derivation of internationally accepted food standards, the Codex Alimentarius Commission has also adopted a *Code of Ethics for International Trade in Food*[3]. This Code was established in recognition of the fact that many developing countries do not yet have the infrastructure to protect their people from food-related health risks and from fraud. The Code seeks to establish standards of ethical conduct for all those engaged in international trade in food.

UK Involvement in the Codex Alimentarius

Throughout the history of the Joint FAO/WHO Food Standards Programme, the UK has played a significant part in the activities of the
Codex Alimentarius Commission and has acted as host government for
the Codex Committee on Sugars and for the Codex Committee on Fats
and Oils. When a Member Country undertakes such a block of work, it
provides the Chairman and all the facilities for the meetings, including
the secretariat and interpretation, at its own expense.

The Commission's rules of procedure apply to all meetings, and its
international staff forms part of the Secretariat of the Committees and
are responsible for the documentation.

The UK contribution is co-ordinated through the Standards Division
of the Ministry of Agriculture, Fisheries and Foods. Delegates to
Codex Committee Meetings represent the United Kingdom and are
expert officials from government departments with relevant responsibilities. The delegates are usually supported by other experts, including
those from the food industry.

Although Codex standards are not introduced directly into UK food
law, they often, nevertheless, have an indirect effect on our legislation.
For example, if the European Commission wishes to make proposals
for new compositional or labelling laws for certain foods, it may well
use a Codex standard (if there is one available) as a suitable basis for
its own proposals. Once these proposals have been adopted as European Directives, they will be implemented into UK legislation, as
already explained.

References

1. Codex Alimentarius Commission *Procedural Manual*, Fifth Edition. FAO/
   WHO, Rome, 1981
2. Codex Alimentarius Commission *Report of the 16th Session of the Joint
   FAO/WHO Codex Alimentarius Commission* held Geneva 1985. FAO/
   WHO, Rome, 1985
3. Codex Alimentarius Commission *Code of Ethics for International Trade in
   Food*. FAO/WHO, Rome, 1980

Part 4

Influences on the System

The United Kingdom system of food legislation is organized in such a manner that the legislation applying at any time is based upon an agreed strategy designed to serve the best interests of consumers and industry alike. This strategy is one in which an attempt is made to achieve a consensus out of what may be seen initially as a situation of conflicts. A similar strategy is inherent in the EEC systems, although here the potential differences may be greater, and not simply those pertaining to the supplier:purchaser interface: the differences more often derive from a desire to preserve the national status quo.

In this section the influences on the system are discussed from two perspectives. First of all, the impact of diet and health considerations is examined in order to illustrate the manner in which one particular influence has served to shape the structure and detail of the UK food laws.

In the second chapter the role of interest groups in general is examined in order to illustrate some key features of the lobbying process.

Impact of concerns about diet and health

One of the primary functions of food legislation is to ensure a safe food supply for the population at large. In fact, the very first section of the *Food Act, 1984*[1] states that it is an offence to treat food in any way that will 'render the food injurious to health'. This concern for the establishment and maintenance of a food supply appropriate to good health has been a feature of food legislation for many years, although it should be stressed that the particular emphasis of concern has changed over the years.

Changes in emphasis

When the Victorian legislators were drafting the provisions of the *Adulteration of Food and Drink Act, 1860*[2], their primary objective was to provide for fair trading by preventing adulteration of foods. The benefits derived from the removal of toxic elements from the nation's basic food supplies was, in many respects, a secondary consideration despite the fact that the issue had been thoroughly researched and publicised by the medical journal, the *Lancet*. However, in this development the achievement of unadulterated foods brought health benefits together with the initially more widely appreciated benefits associated with fair trade.

Later, the development of controls designed to ensure the hygienic quality of food was clearly the result of greater understanding of the relationships between microbial contamination and ill health. Microbial contamination of food and deliberate adulteration of foods with toxic chemicals represent instances in which the food is acting as a vehicle carrying potentially hazardous substances to the consumer. The legislation aims to protect public health by limiting such instances as far as is practicable.

In many ways the measures designed to control the use of food additives follow an essentially similar pattern by mobilizing the current state of toxicological knowledge in order to limit the inclusion into foods of substances which potentially could prove hazardous. The controls have been progressively tightened as scientific knowledge has developed and understanding of the hazards has improved. Furthermore, for many years Ministers have been reminded of the limitation now contained within Section 4 of the *Food Act, 1984*:

> . . . the Ministers shall have regard to the desirability of restricting as far as practicable, the use of substances of no nutritional value as foods or as ingredients of foods.

In this context, the role of the legislation is to maintain the nutritional quality of foodstuffs while limiting such additions to the minimum required to fulfil the particular technological functions.

The nutritional aspects of United Kingdom food legislation have been a central feature since the advent of food policies adopted to maintain the health of the population during the Second World War. It is useful to note from the outset that these nutritional strategies have generally been of a pro-active nature, serving to benefit the health of the population through positive steps requiring action from the food manufacturer and retailer, rather than reactive measures which merely prevent the undesirable.

During the Second World War, the role of food legislation and regulation in the prevention of ill health was developed, beyond that of prevention of infectious disease and poisoning by unsafe ingredients, through the establishment of programmes of fortification with nutrients. Food regulation assumed a more positive role, of disease prevention based on contemporary evaluations of good nutritional practice, rather than simply seeking to limit malpractices associated with adulteration and poor hygiene. This approach is well established nowadays, and today many food manufacturers voluntarily fortify their products with vitamins and minerals in addition to such fortification as is specifically required within the food legislation.

However, nutritional concern in the United Kingdom of the 1980s is no longer restricted to nutrient deficiency and food shortage (except in certain special cases). The emphasis has shifted to the degenerative diseases, in particular, cardiovascular disease, obesity and certain cancers. This shift in emphasis inevitably has an impact on the process of food legislation. This impact is both direct, as calls for specific new legislation are stimulated by concern for public health, and also indirect as the shift in emphasis serves to modify the general climate of opinion towards foods and hence food legislation.

It is worth considering the potential impact of current nutritional thinking on the nation's food legislation, and hence to consider whether selective application of legislation might usefully contribute to the wider efforts designed to lower the incidence of the degenerative diseases. To do so, it is necessary to answer the following questions:

1. What nutritionally motivated legislation exists at present? What was the driving force behind its establishment? Is this still considered to be valid? This principally relates to fortification of foods with vitamins and minerals;
2. What nutritionally motivated legislation could be considered to be worthy of examination in the light of current nutritional advice? How feasible and/or desirable is such a strategy?

Fortification with vitamins and minerals

Fortification of food with vitamins and minerals originated in Britain as a feature of wartime food policy. Food supplies were restricted, and choice limited. Major surveys of nutritional status in the pre-war years had identified widespread nutrient deficiency[3] and fears that restricted supplies would compound this and produce significant nutritional inadequacy led to the fortification of staple commodities. Chief among fortified foods is bread, which has been fortified with calcium continually since 1942. In addition, scientific advances during the 1930s for the first time permitted the mass production of vitamins, most notably thiamin. Amounts of this vitamin were added during 1940–42 to restore that lost during the production of white flours. No white flour was produced during the period 1942–53 but, when production started, thiamin, nicotinic acid and iron were each restored to the flour; as described in Chapter 4, these additions continue. Another food which has been subject to statutory fortification since wartime is margarine, this time with vitamins A and D. These requirements were justified on medical and scientific advice, and have been reviewed from time to time in the post-war years.

The main points to note on the fortification policy are:

1. In the 1930s a shortage of calcium had been detected;
2. Calcium was added to bread to counter a restriction in the supply of dairy produce and milk, the major dietary sources of calcium;
3. Another justification for calcium addition was the raised phytate content of wartime high-extraction flours. Phytate hinders the absorption of calcium from the diet, a factor of potential importance where calcium intake is otherwise restricted;
4. Thiamin, nicotinic acid and iron were (are) added to bread to replace nutrients lost in processing, and are not added to wholemeal flours;
5. Vitamin A fortification of margarine is required at a level equivalent to the amount of vitamin A in the traditional 'yellow fat', namely, butter;
6. Vitamin D fortification of margarine is to a level much higher than the amount in butter.

The most important feature of a fortification and/or supplementation policy is the fact that the entire population has the potential to be at risk of nutrient deficiency. Although a natural variation in requirements exists between individuals, a diet which is deficient in a nutrient inevitably results in a physiological state of ill health. Where deficiency is thought possible for a sizable proportion of the population, then the mass medication achieved by a policy of fortification and/or supplementation is generally thought to be socially desirable.

The British population is today reported to enjoy a generally good state of health with regard to vitamin and/or mineral deficiency, and reports on the composition of breads and the flours from which they are baked have concluded that there is no nutritional advantage in the continued fortification of flour with these or other nutrients[4,5].

However, proposed removal of the requirement to fortify flour was strongly criticized and the consumer pressures have proved sufficient to ensure that fortification will continue.

Mandatory fortification of foods with vitamin D has also been reviewed[6]. The review concluded that the fortification of margarine should continue at present levels, but should not be increased. Mandatory fortification of other foods was not recommended. Voluntary fortification of certain foodstuffs with vitamin D continues to be permitted. Points to note with regard to fortification with vitamin D are as follows:

1. Margarine fortification was implemented to prevent deficiency in the general population at a time of national emergency. Rickets was at that time relatively common in British children;
2. Vitamin D was also made available in the form of supplements and in infant foods;
3. Subsequently, the incidence of rickets fell but did not completely disappear;
4. Rickets have been reported in infants, young children and school children of Asian origin since the early 1970s[7];
5. Osteomalacia was reported during the 1960s, and in subsequent years. It is particularly prevalent in elderly women[8];
6. Suggestions that legislation be amended to extend the range of foods fortified with vitamin D in order to reduce incidence of deficiency amongst those of Asian origin have subsequently been rejected.

Mandatory fortification has also been considered for novel protein foods which are consumed as meat substitutes. The most recent review[9] published in 1980 recommended the supplementation of such foods with thiamin, riboflavin, vitamin B_2, iron and zinc to levels equivalent to those typical of lean pork meat. It should be noted that pork was arbitrarily chosen as typical of meat generally.

Fortification of foods with vitamins, minerals, or other nutrients, is widely used internationally as a means of improving nutritional status and tackling specific nutritional problems associated with deficiency. The particular foods fortified vary from country to country and reflect the national diet and consequently the potential for the prevention of deficiency.

Nutrition in the UK in the 1980s

Vitamins and/or mineral deficiencies are rare among the general public in the UK in the 1980s. However, problems do arise from time to time among specific groups such as immigrants or those in particularly deprived circumstances. However, problems of nutrient deficiency, in general, have been conquered in the UK and today the prevailing nutritional problems are those associated with excess consumption rather than inadequate supply of food. Obesity and overweight are widespread and diet-related disease is common. Cardiovascular disease, in particular, has been identified as having a diet-related aetiology.

In recognition of the diet-related nature of many of the
diseases common in countries such as the UK, recommend.
dietary change have been formulated by many expert group
writing in April 1983, listed 43 reports published around the
since 1968 which advocated a change from the type of diet t)
the UK[10]. Since then, further reviews and recommendations
published. Typical of the recommendations are those prepare,
hoc Working Party of the National Advisory Committee on N ......ıı
Education (NACNE) under the chairmanship of Professor Philip
James. After a certain degree of controversy the group's recommendations were published in September 1983 as a Discussion Paper from the
Health Education Council[11].

The recommended long-term nutritional targets suggested by
NACNE and others are as follows:

1. Energy intakes should be appropriate for the maintenance of optimal body weight;
2. Fat intakes should average no more than 30% of total energy
   intake;
3. Saturated fatty acid intake should average only 10% of total energy
   intake;
4. Average sucrose intake should be lowered to 20 kg per head per
   year;
5. Fibre intake should increase on average to 30 g from 20 g per head
   per day;
6. Desirable to reduce salt intake by an average of 3 g per day;
7. Alcohol intake should decline to 4% of total energy intake.

The NACNE report was followed in July 1984 by a report[12] from the
Committee on Medical Aspects of Food Policy on the subject of *Diet
and Cardiovascular Disease*. The COMA report carried the authority of
an official publication and its main emphasis is related to dietary fats.

> The consumption of saturated fatty acids and of fat in the United
> Kingdom should be decreased . . . The average decrease recom-
> mended for saturated fatty acids is 25 per cent (one quarter). The
> average decrease recommended for fat is 17 per cent (one sixth) at
> the recommended P/S ratio of approximately 0.45 (or 25 per cent
> or one quarter if the current P/S ration of 0.23 is retained).

Informative labelling

The principal legislative recommendation contained within the COMA
report concerned the labelling of foods in order that the public might
have a better understanding of the fat content of particular foods. This
recommendation has been taken up by government: steps have been
taken to establish the most suitable manner of presentation and proposals for new labelling regulations have been published[13].

The COMA panel on cardiovascular disease is not the only advisory
body to have pressed for legislative action with regard to labelling
foods with their fat content. The Food Standards Committee in three
reports published in the early 1980s, made the following comments:

All mince should carry an indication of its fat content by means of a quantitative declaration.[14]

The minimum percentage fat content should be stated on the labels of all types of cream.[15]

All cheeses should bear a declaration of minimum fat content expressed as a percentage of the total weight of the cheese.[16]

The FSC recommendations (above) were motivated principally by nutritional considerations.

In the case of mince, there was an additional concern about the quality and naming of the product on offer in many stores. The FSC review of the (unregulated) mince was somewhat different from the reviews of cream and cheese, for which compositional standards are long established. The FSC did not believe it feasible or desirable to establish a set standard composition which would eliminate the inferior (high fat) mince. The committee's recommendations centred on the provision of more information for the purchaser.

In the case of cream, the present legislation[17] sets out standards for a number of products (single cream, whipping cream, double cream, and so on) each of which is defined with reference to the fat content. The FSC considered that public awareness of the fat content of the different varieties could be improved through clear labelling. Similar considerations applied with respect to cheese. In both of these groups of foods, the established standards define particular products which have recognized qualities.

No action has been taken to introduce fat labelling specifically for mince, cream and cheese, because all three food groups are to be included in the general legislative procedures.

The adoption of more informative labels for meat products (for example) is primarily a means by which superior products may be distinguished from the inferior. However, there was also a recognition in the original advice from the Food Standards Committee[18]—which recommended labelling products with their *lean* meat content—that such labelling would assist the public to make the dietary changes (less fat) advocated in an earlier COMA report on *Diet and Coronary Heart Disease*[19].

Amendment of compositional standards

The very positive development of informative labelling may be contrasted with another potential legislative strategy which has generally been rejected as inappropriate. This alternative strategy could be described as the amendment of compositional standards in order to lower the fat content of particular food items.

At present, a variety of foodstuffs are subject to compositional standards which are defined in terms of minimum fat levels. The list of processed foods includes cheeses[20], butter[21], margarine[22], cream[23], ice-cream[24], salad cream[25] and prepared suet[26]. The only primary product of agriculture which is subject to compositional standard is raw milk which, since 1901, has been presumed genuine only if the fat content is greater than 3.0%[27].

For each of the processed foods cited, the compositional standard serves to protect the name of the product in question; it does not prevent the marketing of a wide variety of alternative products. For example, in the yellow fats sector of the food market, margarine is specifically defined in the *Margarine Regulations, 1967* and the name margarine may be used only for products containing more than 80% fat. This legislation does not hinder the marketing of low-fat spreads (40% fat) or dairy spreads (around 70% fat). Similarly, cheddar cheese must contain a minimum of 48% milk fat in dry matter, but new alternative products which do not use the name 'cheddar cheese' may have a fat content which is considerably lower.

The influence of nutrition on product development is considerable nowadays, and a wide variety of products are marketed specifically on the basis of their nutritional attributes[28]. Many such products are alternatives to traditional foods which are subject to compositional standards.

Long-term UK food policy

It is recognized that informative labelling is the only means through which consumer protection may be maintained at a time of rapid and constant product innovation. A progression towards greater provision of information about foods is a much more feasible proposition than is amendment of compositional requirements. This type of shift is also closer to the principles of long-term UK food policy, which may be surmised from the following quotations:

> It is no part of national food policy to restrict the freedom of the public to choose for themselves what they will eat.

> In connection with diet the role of government is directed towards assembling, assessing and disseminating information based on scientific evidence in the light of which individuals can form their own views and take their own decisions.

The above quotations from the Command Paper *Prevention and Health*[29] may be interpreted as:

1. Freedom of choice;
2. Fewer rather than more statutory compositional controls;
3. Education of the public on nutritional matters;
4. Clear information provided on *all* foods.

To date, this interpretation is an ideal rather than a reality, and it remains difficult for the average consumer to make an informed choice. The progress currently being made with regard to the provisions of nutrition labels on an increasing variety of foods is stimulated as much (if not more) by the commercial considerations of food manufacturers and retailers as by legislative considerations[30].

The current health concerns (as considered by the COMA panel on cardiovascular disease, for example) offer a different perspective on food and health than those underlying earlier considerations which have led to legislative action. Earlier health-related food legislation included four main strategies:

1. Prevention of dangerous adulteration;
2. Action to promote good hygienic practice;
3. Controls on additives which may be used;
4. Programmes of nutritional supplementation.

Each has a common characteristic: each deals with a problem which may affect any or every member of society. Every person is potentially at risk if dangerously adulterated food is eaten or poor hygienic practice followed. Similarly, if a diet is low in one particular vitamin, all persons consuming such a diet will, in time, develop clinical signs of deficiency. In these circumstances, legislators have been willing to adopt strategies which have widespread benefits which can be demonstrated easily.

With respect to the current concerns with respect to (for instance) diet and cardiovascular disease, the situation is by no means so clear cut. The conditions are multifactorial in origin and although it is believed that particular dietary strategies will reduce the risk of developing the condition in question, there can be no guarantee of benefit for each and every person because individual susceptibility varies and, as yet, the available 'evidence falls short of proof'[31]. In recognition of these facts, 'no government has attempted to enforce recommendations relating to nutrition and cardiovascular diseases by direct legislation'[32]. Preference, as stated previously, has been concentrated on education and information rather than specific legislation.

References

1. *Food Act, 1984* (1984 ch 30) HMSO, London. 1984
2. *Adulteration of Food and Drink Act, 1860* Vict (1860 ch 84). HMSO, London. 1860
3. Boyd Orr, J. *Food, Health and Income.* Macmillan, London. 1936
4. Ministry of Agriculture, Fisheries and Food *Food Standards Committee Second Report on Bread and Flour* FSC/REP/61. HMSO, London. 1974
5. Department of Health and Social Security *Nutritional Aspects of Bread and Flour. Report of the Panel on Bread, Flour and other Cereal Products. Committee on Medical Aspects of Food Policy.* Report on Health and Social Subjects No 23. HMSO, London. 1981
6. Department of Health and Social Security *Rickets and Osteomalacia. Report of the Working Party on Fortification of Food with Vitamin D Committee on Medical Aspects of Food Policy.* Report on Health and Social Subjects No 19. HMSO, London. 1980
7. *Rickets and Osteomalacia* op.cit. (reference 6) Section 3.5
8. *Rickets and Osteomalacia* op.cit. (reference 6) Section 3.3
9. Department of Health and Social Security *Foods Which Simulate Meat: The Nutritional Aspects of Vegetable Protein Foods which are Meat Analogues. Report of the Panel on Novel Foods. Committee on Medical Aspects of Food Policy.* Report on Health and Social Subjects No 17. HMSO, London. 1980
10. Truswell, A. S. *The Development of Dietary Guidelines. Food Technology in Australia,* **35**, 498–502. 1983

11. NACNE *ad hoc* Working Party *A Discussion Paper on Proposals for Nutritional Guidelines for Health Education in Britain.* Health Education Council, London. 1983
12. Department of Health and Social Security *Diet and Cardiovascular Disease. Report of the Panel on Diet in Relation to Cardiovascular Disease Committee on Medical Aspects of Food Policy.* Report on Health and Social Subjects No 28. HMSO, London. 1984
13. First announced as follows: Michael Jopling (Minister for Agriculture, Fisheries and Food) Written Answer to Sir Peter Mills, Question on *Food Labelling. Hansard* 6th Series Vol 75, col 79–81. 12 March 1985
14. Ministry of Agriculture, Fisheries and Food. *Food Standards Committee Report on Mince* FSC/REP/77. HMSO, London. 1983
15. Ministry of Agriculture, Fisheries and Food *Food Standards Committee Report on Cream* FSC/REP/76. HMSO, London. 1982
16. Ministry of Agriculture, Fisheries and Food *Food Standards Committee Report on Cheese* FSC/REP/75. HMSO, London. 1982
17. *Cream Regulations, 1970* SI No 752. HMSO, London. 1970
18. Ministry of Agriculture, Fisheries and Food *Food Standards Committee Report on Meat Products* FSC/REP/72. HMSO, London. 1980
19. Department of Health and Social Security *Diet and Coronary Heart Disease. Report of the Advisory Panel of the Committee on Medical Aspects of Food Policy (Nutrition) on Diet in Relation to Cardiovascular and Cerebrovascular Disease.* Report on Health and Social Subjects No 7. HMSO, London. 1974
20. *Cheese Regulations, 1970* SI No 94. HMSO, London. 1970
21. *Butter Regulations, 1966* SI No 1074. HMSO, London. 1966
22. *Margarine Regulations, 1967* SI No 1867. HMSO, London. 1967
23. *Cream Regulations, 1966* op.cit. (reference 17)
24. *Ice Cream Regulations, 1967* SI No 1866. HMSO, London. 1967
25. *Salad Cream Regulations, 1966* SI No 1051. HMSO, London. 1967
26. *Food Standards (Suet) Order, 1952* SI No 2203. HMSO, London. 1952
27. *Sale of Milk Regulations, 1901* SR&O No 657. HMSO, London. 1901
28. Slattery J. *Diet/Health: Food Industry Initiatives.* Briefing Paper Series. Food Policy Research, University of Bradford, Bradford. 1986
29. Department of Health and Social Security/Department of Education and Science/Scottish Office/Welsh Office *Prevention and Health* Cmnd 7047. HMSO, London. 1977
30. Freckleton, A. *Who is Shaping the Nutritional Label?* Briefing Paper Series. Food Policy Research, University of Bradford, Bradford. 1985
31. Acheson, E. D. (Chief Medical Officer, Department of Health and Social Security; Chairman, Committee on Medical Aspects of Food Policy) *Preface* to COMA Report on *Diet and Cardiovascular Disease* (op.cit., reference 12)
32. COMA Report on *Diet and Cardiovascular Disease* (op.cit., reference 12)

10 Role of interest groups

Throughout this book, reference has been made to the various opportunities for interested parties to make their views known to those responsible for the administration and development of the nation's food legislation. These opportunities exist at every stage, from the informal consultations and communications which take place before an issue is considered for review, through to the formal processes of consultation which are required under section 188 of the *Food Act, 1984*[1] before new standards regulations may be laid before Parliament.

Each review, in theory, offers many opportunities for a wide variety of interested organizations to make their views known to government and to its officials. However, the point can be made that the review process takes place away from general notice and thus it may be difficult for many, potentially very interested, groups and organizations to know that this opportunity exists. Moreover, there is a question of timing because, once any review process has been initiated, it is essential that evidence be submitted at the key times when impact can be maximized: it is of no use to submit evidence to an advisory committee after it has taken its decisions and made its recommendations; similarly, it is of little value providing an advisory committee with information on topics outside its brief.

The review process

Briefly examining the basic review process again, a few pointers for effective submission of evidence can be noticed.

Initiation

To initiate a review of legislation, whether deemed necessary from a consumer perspective or from that of the food industry, it is necessary to gain allies. Key individuals are MPs and the Press, who can ask appropriate questions and publicize the 'need' for change. Also important are the Ministers and their departments, as they must be convinced of the need for change and be aware of the pressures for change.

Committee review

If a topic is referred to an advisory committee, this will be reported in the Press, although not generally in the popular Press. The committee will be given a specific topic for examination and will seek information *relevant* to this. To be particularly effective it is necessary to be aware fully of the subject being investigated — this is generally outlined in the Press notice from the Ministry — and to present relevant evidence before the date given. However, in many instances, if a general statement of interest and reference to the form of detailed comment to be provided is made at this stage, a committee will receive late submissions or will invite further evidence.

Comments on report

Committee reports are simply advice to Ministers and, as such, are not statements of government policy. If there are points within a report with which an organization *agrees or disagrees*, it has the opportunity to make them known to the committee and to government. 'Agree or disagree' is stressed above, as is likely that those agreeing with a report will not comment, whereas those disagreeing will react and will make their views known.

Proposals and draft regulations

These are drafted by officials within the appropriate Ministry and comments are invited from 'interested parties', as required by Section 118 of the *Food Act*. A mailing list of interested parties is drawn up to include those organizations who have specifically asked to be included, together with commercial organizations directly concerned with those products which may be subject to any new legislation.

The best way for any organization to keep fully informed of what is taking place is to be on the Ministries' mailing lists to receive information as it is released.

Again, any evidence and comments should be submitted before the dates declared with proposals and drafts. At all stages, information may be sent either to the responsible Minister or to the department concerned, or to both! In the case of points raised in an advisory committee report, information may also be sent directly to the committee chairman.

At each stage in the proceedings MPs may be able to assist to make views known, either by asking appropriate questions of Ministers in Parliament, by contributing to debates on primary legislation or by 'praying' against subordinate legislation when it is presented to Parliament.

Organizations submitting evidence

At most stages in the development or amendment of the United Kingdom's food legislation it is not possible to identify which organizations have contributed evidence or commentary. One key exception to this general rule is where an issue is subjected to review by the Food

Advisory Committee. This Committee — like its predecessors, the Food Standards Committee and the Food Additives and Contaminants Committee — includes in its reports a list of those providing information; as stated before, the nature of this evidence is not disclosed.

Tables 10.1, 10.2 and *10.3* list as examples those submitting evidence to the Food Standards Committee review of meat products (report published in 1980[2]), to the Food Standards Committee review of water in food (report published 1978[3]) and the Food Advisory Committee review of coated and ice-glazed fish products (report published 1987[4]). From the three tables it may be seen that those submitting evidence are categorized into four groups:

1. Trade interests;
2. Enforcement interests;
3. Consumer organizations;
4. Others.

Similarly, it may be noted that the majority of submissions are provided by organizations rather than (for example) individual firms.

If each main category is considered in turn, a number of key points can be identified:

Trade interests

Here three main levels of presentation can be identified:

1. Individual company;
2. Sectoral associations;
3. Associations representing entire food industry.

Evidence from individual companies is, for most reviews, relatively rare. Most companies prefer to leave presentation of evidence to the appropriate trade associations; in fact, many would regard a requirement for individual companies to become directly involved as a failure to present a united approach. In general, individual companies become involved only where special circumstances apply to their products.

Most submissions are provided by associations representing the interests of particular sections of the food industry. Examples of such organizations include:

1. Dairy Trade Federation;
2. Bacon and Meat Manufacturers' Association;
3. British Frozen Food Federation;
4. Federation of Bakers;
5. Cocoa, Chocolate and Confectionery Alliance.

Each of the sectoral trade associations will take the lead in presenting its members' views to government. The sectoral trade associations vary in strength and resources but generally comprise a small headquarters staff supported by a network of committees made up of industry representatives. The larger associations are able to employ specialist staff who are able to maintain contact with the appropriate officials in both the United Kingdom and the EEC.

Table 10.1   List of organizations and individuals submitting evidence to the Food Standards Committee Review of Meat Products

Organizations and individual firms associated with food production

Albright and Wilson Ltd
G. W. Anstee
Association of British Abattoir Owners Ltd
Bacon and Meat Manufacturers Association
British Bacon Curers Federation
British Food Manufacturing Industries Research Association
British Poultry Meat Association
British Soya Products Ltd
Brooke Bond Oxo Ltd
Cadbury Schweppes Foods Ltd
Courtaulds Ltd
Deltec Foods Ltd
Devro Ltd
The Distillers Company Ltd
Dornay Foods Ltd
EEC Seed Crushers' and Oil Processors' Federation
Flour Milling and Baking Research Association
Food Manufacturers' Federation
H. J. Heinz and Company Ltd
The Lane Food Company Ltd
Libby, McNeil and Libby Ltd
Lovell and Christmas (Northern) Ltd
Marks and Spencer Ltd
Meat and Livestock Commission
McAuley Edwards Ltd
National Association of Wholesale Meat Salesmen of Scotland
National Association of Master Bakers, Confectioners and Caterers
National Federation of Meat Traders
Natural Sausage Casings Association
The Nestlé Company Ltd
Provision Importers Association
Rank Hovis McDougall Ltd
Sello-Bollans Ltd
Shippams Ltd
Tesco Stores Ltd
UK Association of Frozen Food Producers
Unilever Ltd
Universe Foods Ltd
Wander Ltd
Warburtons Ltd
Westler Foods Ltd

Enforcement authorities and related interests

Association of County Councils of Scotland
Association of District Councils
Association of Public Analysts
Borders Regional Council
A C Bushnell Esq., Public Analyst, Lancashire County Council
Corporation of Glasgow
County of Cleveland

Durham County Council
Dyfed County Council
Edinburgh Corporation
Gloucester County Council
Greater Manchester Council
Hampshire County Council
A J Harrison Esq, Chief Scientific Adviser, County of Avon
Hereford and Worcester County Council
Hertfordshire County Council
Institute of Trading Standards Administration
London Borough of Islington
London Borough of Redbridge
Merseyside County Council
Mid-Glamorgan County Council
Moir and Palgrave, Public Analysts
Muter and Hackman, Public Analysts
Northants County Council
Nottingham County Council
Royal Borough of Kensington and Chelsea
Salop County Council
J. H. Shelton Esq., Public Analyst
South Yorkshire County Council
Staffordshire County Council
Warwickshire County Council
West Midland County Council

Consumers and representative organizations

Consumers' Association
Consumer Association of South Humberside
Consumer Forum of Greater Manchester
Eastcote Womens' Institute
National Federation of Consumer Groups
Parliamentary Committee Co-operative Union Ltd

Other interests

British Nutrition Foundation
Douglas R. S. Haigh Esq., Food Standards and Labelling Consultant
W. J. Hogan Esq.
Institute of Food Science and Technology
Mrs D. Kilner
National Farmers' Union
Union International Research Centre
Woman
Zoological Society of London

Table 10.2   List of organizations and individuals submitting evidence to the Food Standards Committee Review of Water in Food

Organizations associated with food production or distribution

Albright and Wilson Ltd
Alginate Industries Ltd
Association of Butter Blenders and Butter and Cheese Packers
AVAB (Automatic Vending Association of Britain)
Bakers' Union
Baxters Ltd
British Association of Canned Food Importers and Distributors
British Bacon Curers Federation
British Bakels Ltd
British Food Manufacturing Industries Research Association
British Oatmeal Millers Association
British Poultry Federation Ltd
British Poultry Meat Association Ltd
British Soft Drinks Council
British Soya Products Ltd
British Sugar Refiners' Association
Cake and Biscuit Alliance Ltd
The Cocoa, Chocolate and Confectionery Alliance
Coffee Trade Federation
Dairy Trade Federation
Federation of Bakers
Flour Milling and Baking Research Association
Food Manufacturers' Federation Inc
Glaxo Laboratories Ltd
Honeywill-Atlas Ltd
Ice Cream Federation Ltd
London Chamber of Commerce and Industry (Canned Food Trade Section)
Margarine and Shortening Manufacturers' Association
Marks and Spencer Ltd
Meat Manufacturers' Association
Multiple Food and Drink Retailers Association
National Association of British and Irish Millers Ltd
National Association of Cider Makers
National Association of Creamery Proprietors and Wholesale Dairymen
   (Incorporated)
National Association of Master Bakers, Confectioners and Caterers
Ormeau Bakery Ltd, Belfast
Provision Importers' Association
Retail Consortium
Rowntree Mackintosh Ltd
Scotch Whisky Association
Scottish Union of Bakers and Allied Workers
Self Raising Flour Association
Tate and Lyle Refineries Ltd
UK Association of Frozen Food Producers
Van den Berghs and Jurgens Ltd
Vinegar Brewers' Federation

Associations of Local Authorities and of officers associated with enforcement

Association of County Councils
Association of County Councils in Scotland
Association of District Councils
Association of Public Analysts
Buckinghamshire County Council
A. C. Bushnell Esq., Public Analyst, Lancashire County Council
County of Cleveland, County Consumer Protection Officer
Essex County Council, County Consumer and Public Protection Officer
Greater Manchester Council
Hampshire County Council
Institute of Trading Standards Administration
Kensington and Chelsea Royal Borough Council
Moir and Palgrave, Public Analysts
Muter and Hackman, Public Analysts
North East Regional Analytical Service
Nottinghamshire County Council
Scottish Counties of Cities Association
South Yorkshire County Council
Staffordshire County Council Analyst's Department

Consumers and representative organizations

Consumers' Association
Miss D. M. Hawes (Senior Lecturer in Rural Home Economics, Bucks
    Federation of Women's Institutes)
Huntingdon and Peterborough Federation of Women's Institutes
National Federation of Consumer Groups
Parliamentary Committee Co-operative Union Ltd
Plymouth Consumer Groups
Mary Reynbolds, Consultant Home Economist

Other individuals and organizations

Food Research Institute
W. J. Hogan Esq.
J. Irons Esq.
Institute of Food Science and Technology
R. Kempton Esq.
Laboratory of the Government Chemist
National Farmers' Union
P. J. Rowe Esq.
Torry Research Station
Woman

Table 10.3   List of organizations submitting evidence to the Food Advisory Committee review of coated and ice-glazed products

Trade interests

British Retailers' Association
Co-operative Union Ltd Parliamentary Committee
Dawnfresh Seafoods Ltd
National Federation of Fish Friers Ltd
United Kingdom Association of Frozen Food Products

Consumer organizations

Consumers' Association

Enforcement authorities

Cheshire County Council, Department of Trading Standards
Cumbria County Council, Department of Trading Standards
Institute of Trading Standards Administration
Local Authorities Co-ordinating Body on Trading Standards
Lancashire County Council, County Analyst's Laboratory
Southwark Public Protection Department
South Yorkshire County Council
Tyne and Wear County Council, Consumer Services Department
West Yorkshire Metropolitan County Council

Other interests

Davtech Food and Medical Consultancy

In addition to the sectoral associations, there is also the Food and Drink Federation (formerly the Food and Drink Industries Council and the Food Manufacturers' Federation). This organization exists to provide an industry-wide representation into decision-making in both the UK and the EEC. The FDF is principally involved in those issues which relate to the entire food industry, rather than those which will affect only particular sectors. Thus, the FDF was not directly involved in the Food Advisory Committee review of coated and ice-glazed fish products (cited earlier) but would have an interest in matters such as labelling of foods or food irradiation, because such measures can be seen to have a common impact on the operation of the entire industry. In addition to its role representing the interests of the wider food industry, the FDF also provides secretariat facilities for 36 of the smaller trade associations such as the British Pasta Products Association and the Pre-Packed Flour Association.

The Retail Consortium provides a similar service for member companies in the retailing sector.

Enforcement interests

Legislation is of value only if it is enforceable. In the UK, enforcement is chiefly the responsibility of trading standards officers and environmental health officers employed by county and/or district authorities. These officials, in addition, provide advice to the food industries on the interpretation of food legislation. Where a breach of the legislation is suspected, samples of food will be analysed at the public analyst's laboratory. In the course of their work officials identify many instances where changes to legislation are desirable: hence, these professions provide a major input to the development of new or amended legislation. For both professions, submissions may be made either by individual authorities or by the professional associations — the Institute of Trading Standards Administration, the Institution of Environmental Health Officers and the Association of Public Analysts. As stated previously with reference to industry evidence, a co-ordinated approach offers distinct advantages over individual submissions. In the case of enforcement bodies, the existence of the professional organizations provides the opportunity to collect samples of food from many parts of the country, to subject these samples to a standardized testing procedure and then to present evidence to government on the basis of a nation-wide study, rather than merely relying on information gathered in one locality. Nation-wide evidence of a problem is much more likely to result in government action than is evidence solely from one town or county.

Consumer organizations

The consumer viewpoint is principally represented by organizations such as the Consumers' Association, National Consumer Council and Consumers in the European Community Group. Here, too a co-ordinated approach is generally followed. The Consumers' Association has regularly contributed evidence and periodically reviews food legislation subjects in its magazine (*Which*), in which it invites observations from members.

While national consumer organizations regularly contribute to the legislative process, it is fair to note that local groups have also made their views known. This has particularly been the case when issues relating to the labelling of food (see *Food Standards Committee Second Report on Food Labelling*[5] or *Food Standards Committee Report on the Date Marking of Food*[6]) have been discussed. The Food Standards Committee review of claims and misleading descriptions[7] (conducted concurrently with the review of labelling) similarly attracted a greater level of interest than is usual when the legislation relating to a specific food item is considered. However, consumer input into the legislative process is generally restricted by the fact that groups may be unaware of the review or without the technical expertise of either industry or enforcement bodies. A strong case can be made for encouraging further informed consumer input into the legislative processes.

Other interests

Almost by definition, this group draws on a very wide cross-section of the community including:

1. Organizations representing professional groups with an interest in food, such as the British Dietetic Association or the Institute of Food Science and Technology;
2. Government scientific and research establishments, such as the Food Research Institute, Torry Research Station or the Laboratory of the Government Chemist;
3. University departments or individual academics;
4. The media; for example, the magazine *Woman* has submitted evidence on behalf of its readers.

Collaboration

Throughout the various stages leading to revised legislation the value of collaboration is recognized, with associations having considerably greater resources and influence than individuals or even individual smaller groups.

The value of organization into a structured entity has been recognized by those who favour a change in the controls relating to food additives. The Food Additives Campaign Team (FACT) is a coalition of many organizations and individuals seeking to limit the use of food additives in Britain. FACT comprises over 20 national organizations, including:

1. National Federation of Women's Groups;
2. General, Municipal and Boilermakers' Union;
3. British Dietetic Association;
4. Coronary Prevention Group;
5. Campaign for Freedom of Information;
6. London Food Commission.

In addition, FACT has gained political support from MPs of all parties, and has been able to attract considerable publicity for its campaign. This organization is a very good example of how an energetic campaigning group is able to attract attention to its aims and to gather support. The issue of food additive use is thus less likely to be viewed as a minority issue but rather as one requiring serious government attention.

EEC considerations

So far in this chapter, discussion has centred on the role of interest groups within the United Kingdom. The activity is paralleled in Brussels with respect to European deliberations. Each of the key groups — industry, consumers, enforcement — provides an input into European decision-making. This is either at a direct level, where UK organizations make their views known to both UK government representatives in Brussels and EEC officials, or at an indirect level, where UK organizations provide an input into European organizations which make sectoral views known to EEC officials. For example, UK consumer organizations will operate in collaboration with consumer groups from other EEC Member States under the umbrella organization Bureau European des Unions de Consommateurs.

Similarly, the industry view will be put forward by the Federation des Industries Agricôle et Alimentaires (Federation of Agriculture and Food Industries), which will seek to present a case which represents the common interest of the European Food Industry as a whole. Where an issue affects only one sector of the food industry, then a sectoral association will seek to present a European consensus view for that particular industry. For example, the Federation de l'industrie de l'huilerie de la CEE, which has a membership of national associations relating to the production and distribution of edible oils, or the Flour Milling Associations Group of the EEC Countries which has a membership of national associations relating to flour milling, will each provide a co-ordinated input from the named industries.

In many instances, the views of a nation's consumers and industry will coincide and in this case the national interest is communicated by the permanent representatives of that nation in Brussels. The adoption of the *Single European Act*[8] and the simplified procedures outlined in Chapter 7 and *Appendix 2* now means that it is no longer sufficient to rely on the ability of national representatives to hold back legislation through the use of a veto. In future it will be increasingly necessary to work through the auspices of pan-European organizations when wishing to influence the course of legislation. This will be particularly the case as the main centre of power in this context shifts from national administrations to Europe.

References

1. *Food Act, 1984* Eliz 2 (1984 ch 30). HMSO, London. 1984
2. Ministry of Agriculture, Fisheries and Food *Food Standards Committee Report on Meat Products* FSC/REP/72. HMSO, London. 1980
3. Ministry of Agriculture, Fisheries and Food *Food Standards Committee Report on Water in Food* FSC/REP/70. HMSO, London. 1978
4. Ministry of Agriculture, Fisheries and Food *Food Advisory Committee Report on Coated and Ice-Glazed Fish Products* FdAC/REP/3. HMSO, London. 1987

5. Ministry of Agriculture, Fisheries and Food *Food Standards Committee Second Report on Food Labelling* FSC/REP/69. HMSO, London. 1979
6. Ministry of Agriculture, Fisheries and Food *Food Standards Committee Report on the Date Marking of Food* FSC/REP/59. HMSO, London. 1972
7. Ministry of Agriculture, Fisheries and Food *Food Standards Committee Report on Claims and Misleading Descriptions*, FSC/REP/71. HMSO, London. 1980
8. *Single European Act* signed at Luxembourg on 17 February 1986 and at The Hague, 28 February 1986. Published in Council of the European Communities *Single European Act and Final Act*. Office for Official Publications of the European Communities, Luxembourg. 1986

Part 5

Concluding Comments

1 Summary and overview

This book has set out to illustrate the workings of the Food Legislative System of the UK; in order to do so, reference has been made to a number of advisory bodies, and to numerous examples of food legislation past, present and proposed. It is the nature of any publication such as this, that the material included will, in certain circumstances, become outdated or even replaced. This is an inevitable consequence of new developments: the law is not a static entity, but is continually evolving to take account of these new developments.

As reported elsewhere, the intention has not been to include each and every amendment or redraft of every item of food legislation, but rather to illustrate the mechanisms through which change is achieved and the points at which there is opportunity for interested parties to make their views known to the decision makers.

At the time of writing, a number of new legislative provisions are under discussion, both in the UK itself and in the EEC:

1. Government has been advised by the Food Advisory Committee to introduce controls over the composition and labelling of certain specific fish products[1];
2. Proposals have been published for the amendment of the existing legislation relating to the use of colours in food[2], following a report from the Food Advisory Committee[3];
3. Government has been advised that the use of irradiation as a method of food preservation would present no hazard to health, and that legislation should be amended to permit the use of this process for foods consumed by the general public[4];
4. The EEC has published documents[5–9] outlining suggested changes to the existing EEC legislation as part of its wider programme of work towards the establishment of a truly Common Market in foodstuffs[10].

For each of the above issues there will be debate which will be more or less heated, depending on the degree of controversy or publicity associated with the issue. For example, the consideration of whether or not any compositional standard be introduced for fish fingers will attract relatively little attention, whereas the issue of food irradiation will be much more contentious, with many more organizations and individuals contributing to the debate; the scale of interest may be gauged by the fact that by October 1986, around 4600 individuals and 117 organizations had provided comments to government following the publication of the Advisory Committee's report[11]. This degree of interest is likely to continue if (as is thought probable) proposals for new legislation are published in due course by the EEC.

The number of sets of comments relating to irradiation of foods is not solely indicative of the level of public concern: it undoubtedly also reflects the misunderstanding of the legislative system by many of those who reported the publication of the Advisory Committee's report as a statement of final policy on this issue.

It is hoped that, through this book, understanding of the system will have been improved and hence balanced and informed comment will be provided to the legislators and their officials at each of the stages in the evolution of any item of food legislation. It is possible for the UK (and the EEC) to be provided with sound legislation (on food and other issues) only if decision makers have available all the relevant facts, together with an indication of the degree of public and administrative concern.

References

1. Ministry of Agriculture, Fisheries and Food *Food Advisory Committee Report on Coated and Ice-Glazed Fish Products*. FdAC/REP/3. HMSO, London. 1987
2. Ministry of Agriculture, Fisheries and Food *Amendment of the Colouring Matter in Food Regulations*. Draft Proposals. 21 April 1987
3. Ministry of Agriculture, Fisheries and Food *Food Advisory Committee Final Report on the Review of the Colouring Matter in Food Regulations, 1973* FdAC/REP/4. HMSO, London. 1987
4. Department of Health and Social Security *Advisory Committee on Irradiated and Novel Foods Report on the Safety and Wholesomeness of Irradiated Foods*. HMSO, London. 1986
5. Commission of the European Communities *Proposals for a Council Directive on the Approximation of the Laws of Member States concerning Food Additives Authorised for Use in Foodstuffs Intended for Human Consumption* COM (86) 87 final. *Official Journal of the European Communities* C116/2. 16 May 1986
6. Commission of the European Communities *Proposal for a Council Directive amending Directive 79/112/EEC on the Approximation of the laws of the Member States relating to the Labelling, Preparation and Advertising of Foodstuffs for Sale to the Ultimate Consumer* COM (86) 89 final. *Official Journal of the European Communities* C124/06. 23 May 1986
7. Commission of the European Communities *Proposal for a Council Directive on the Approximation of the laws of the Member States relating to Materials and Articles Intended to Come into Contact with Foodstuffs* COM (86) 90 final. *Official Journal of the European Communities* C124/07. 23 May 1986
8. Commission of the European Communities *Proposal for a Council Directive on the Approximation of the laws of the Member States relating to Foodstuffs Intended for Particular Nutritional Uses* COM (86) 91 final. *Official Journal of the European Communities* C124/06 91. 23 May 1986

9. Commission of the European Communities *Proposals for a Council Directive on the Official Inspection of Foodstuffs* COM (86) 747 final. *Official Journal of the European Communities* C20/6. 27 January 1987

10. Commission of the European Communities *Completion of the Internal Market: Community Legislation on Foodstuffs*. Communication from the Commission to the Council and to the European Parliament. COM (85) 603 final. Office for Official Publications of the European Communities, Luxembourg. 1985

11. Currie, E. (Parliamentary Secretary, Department of Health and Social Security) Written Answer to Reginald Freeson. Question on *Irradiated Food. Hansard* 6th Series, Vol 102 col 978. 23 October 1986

Appendix 1   The *Food Act, 1984*: Arrangement of Sections

Part 1   Food Generally

Composition and Labelling of Food

1. Offences as to preparation and sale of injurious foods
2. General protection for purchasers of food
3. Defences in proceedings under s 2
4. Regulations as to composition of food etc
5. Ministers' power to obtain particulars of ingredients
6. Food falsely described
7. Regulations as to describing food

Food Unfit for Human Consumption

8. Sale etc of unfit food
9. Examination and seizure of suspected food
10. Food as prizes etc
11. Food in transit
12. Products of knackers' yards

Hygiene

13. Regulations as to food hygiene
14. Court's power to disqualify caterer
15. Byelaws as to food

Registration of Premises and Licensing of Vehicles

16. Registration: ice-cream, sausages etc
17. Extension of s 16 to other businesses
18. Application for registration
19. Refusal or cancellation of registration
20. Regulations for licensing vehicles, stalls etc

Part II   Milk, Dairies and Cream Substitutes

Part VII   General and Supplemental

Acquisition of Land, and Orders to Permit Works

Inquiries and Default

Protection

Subordinate Legislation

Notices, Forms and Continuances

Expenses and Receipts

Interpretation and Operation

Schedules

Appendix 2   Notes on the European Economic Community and the operation of its institutions

Establishment and objectives of the EEC

The European Economic Community (EEC) was established after the signing of the *Treaty of Rome*[1] (formally referred to as the *Treaty Establishing the European Economic Community* or *EEC Treaty*) by the six founding countries (Belgium, France, West Germany, Italy, Luxembourg, Netherlands) on 25 March 1957. The principal objective, central to the establishment of the EEC, is to bring closer together the relationships existing between the Member States. This political objective is implemented through the implementation of four economic objectives:

1. Harmonious development of economic activities;
2. Continuous and balanced expansion;
3. Increase in stability;
4. Accelerated raising of the standard of living.

Throughout its activities, the EEC seeks to establish a common internal market comprising all member states, and has adopted a number of policies to this end. The Common Agricultural Policy (CAP) is one such policy and its objectives are set out in Article 39 of the *Treaty of Rome*.

The EEC has been enlarged on three occasions since 1957 with the accession of six further Member States:

1. Denmark   1973
2. Ireland   1973
3. United Kingdom   1973
4. Greece   1981
5. Portugal   1986
6. Spain   1986

United Kingdom accession to the EEC was accomplished through an Act of Accession and was set out in the *European Communities Act, 1972*[2].

Institutions established by the EEC

The EEC has established a number of institutions, the major roles of which are set out below.

Council

Made up of Ministers from each Member State, the Council is the highest decision-making body in the EEC. Member States delegate Ministers to attend relevant meetings: meetings of a political nature or of general Community interest are attended by Ministers of Foreign Affairs while specialist meetings are attended by the appropriate Minister — for example, those relating to food or agriculture are attended by the Minister for Agriculture, Fisheries and Food. Several Council Meetings may be in session concurrently.

Meetings of the Council are presided over by the Minister representing the Member State currently President. The office of President rotates amongst Member States with terms of six months. The President serves as representative of Member States and as chief spokesperson of the Community.

The Council is supported in its work by a system of committees staffed by Community civil servants and other officials. Presidency of the Council involves a major increase in work-load for senior civil servants working within the domestic Ministries as the Presidential State seeks to conclude a programme of work during its term of office.

Decisions are generally taken by a qualified majority. Weightings are as follows:

Belgium:	5
Denmark:	3
France:	10
Germany:	10
Greece:	5
Ireland:	3
Italy:	10
Luxembourg:	2
Netherlands:	5
Portugal:	5
Spain:	8
United Kingdom:	10

A qualified majority of 54 votes is required to act upon a proposal, with the agreement of at least seven member states. However, unanimity is usually sought in the decision-making process and the power of veto is recognized for some matters.

The decision-making process within the Council was modified in 1986 by the *Single European Act*[3] which amended the *Treaty Establishing the*

European Economic Community (Treaty of Rome). Article 149 of the
Treaty of Rome required that the Council achieve unanimity when
amending (or rejecting) any proposals from the Commission (q.v.). The
Single European Act, introduced into United Kingdom law by the
European Communities (Amendment) Act, 1986[4], brought about the
possibility of action by qualified majority. The first step was the introduction of a co-operation procedure whereby consultation with the
Assembly (q.v.) is replaced by 'co-operation with the European Parliament'.

The sequence of events is now broadly as follows:

1. The Council will obtain the opinion of the European Parliament on
    proposals from the Commission. The Council will then reach a
    decision by qualified majority; this will be accepted as a Common
    Position.
2. The Council's Common Position will be communicated to the
    European Parliament, together with the reasons behind the deci-
    sion. The European Parliament will also be informed of the Com-
    mission position.
3. The European Parliament will take a decision approving or other-
    wise of the Common Position. Three possibilities follow:

    (c) Approval by European Parliament. The Council will now act
         definitively on the Common Position. (This also applies if the
         European Parliament fails to reach a decision within a stated
         period of time — usually three months.)
    (b) Rejection of the Council's Common Position by an absolute
         majority of the European Parliament. The Council must now
         reach unanimity before any new measures may be introduced.
    (c) The European Parliament may make amendments to the pro-
         posal. The proposal is re-examined by the Commission which
         may accept the amendments, in which case, the Council may
         adopt the amended proposal by qualified majority. If the
         Council wishes to introduce further amendments into this re-
         vised proposal, unanimity is required. If the European Parlia-
         ment's amendments are not accepted by the Commission, an
         opinion will be expressed to the Council which must decide
         unanimously on whether or not to accept the amendments.

Proposals for the approximation (harmonization) of laws (including
food-related laws) made previously under Article 100 of the *Treaty of
Rome* may now be made under a new Article, 100A, which includes
the co-operation procedures outlined above.

The overall effect of the changes described above is to move away
from a situation in which any Member State may block legislation
unilaterally to protect its national interests.

Commission

The Commission has four basic roles:

1. To ensure the implementation of the various treaties which
    establish and maintain the Community;

2. To initiate recommendations and co-ordinate policy on matters contained in the Treaties on a Community-wide basis;
3. To have the power of decision on certain matters and to participate in the shaping of measures agreed by the Council;
4. To act as the executive body of the Community.

With regard to food-related legislation, it is the second of these roles which is of greatest importance. The Commission develops policy options and makes recommendations to the Council and to Member States. The harmonization of rules and regulations is a significant function of the Commission.

The Commission *per se* comprises 17 Commissioners, including at least one but not more than two nationals of each Member State. Commissioners are required to be completely independent of national governments and to act as representatives of the Community as a whole. Each Commissioner has responsibility for one or more Directorates General (the Community equivalents of Ministries in a national administration).

The Assembly

The Assembly, more commonly referred to nowadays as the European Parliament, is not directly involved in proposing new legislation, and as such is quite different from national Parliaments. Its function is mainly advisory and supervisory although, as has been noted above, an apparently greater role has been given to the European Parliament following the *Single European Act*. However, the European Parliament's views may always be overturned by the Council.

Members are elected by direct elections held every five years. The allocation of seats between Member States is broadly in line with population distribution:

Belgium:	24
Denmark:	16
France:	81
Germany:	81
Greece:	24
Ireland:	15
Italy:	81
Luxembourg:	6
Netherlands:	25
Portugal:	24
Spain:	60
United Kingdom:	81
Total:	518

The chief function of the Parliament with regard to food-related legislation is to comment and advise on proposals from the Commission. In addition, Members of the European Parliament may direct parliamentary questions to the Commission to gain information and/or inform the Commission of topics of concern.

The only real power given to the Assembly is the right to force the resignation of the Commission as a body through a motion of censure. This power has never been exercised.

Economic and Social Committee

This body is constitued as an advisory body and comprises 156 members, representing a cross-section of economic interests (industrialists, trade unions, consumers)[5]. Members are appointed in an individual capacity by the Council and care is taken to balance the various economic and social categories. A list of representatives from the UK is given in *Table A2.1*. Members are drawn from all Member States as follows:

Belgium:	12
Denmark:	9
France:	24
Germany:	24
Greece:	12
Ireland:	9
Italy:	24
Luxembourg:	6
Netherlands	12
Portugal	12
Spain:	21
United Kingdom:	24

The Committee is primarily a consultative body although it has the right to initiate policy on its own initiative.

On certain issues the requirement for the Council and Commission to consult the Economic and Social Committee is specifically stated in Community treaties. With regard to food legislation, such an obligation exists with regard to regulations or directives made under *Article 100* of the *Treaty of Rome* which refers to the approximation of laws. This obligation continues in Article 100A.

Opinions from the Economic and Social Committee are not binding on the Council or Commission, although there is an acknowledgement that such opinions constitute sound and informed views.

Court of Justice

The Court's role is to ensure that the law is observed in the interpretation and application of the various treaties which established the Community. The objective is to ensure that there is uniform application of Community law. Actions may be taken against Member States by the Commission or other Member States to ensure compliance with the treaties. Actions may be brought by individuals and organizations against national governments and any of their institutions.

The Court itself is constituted of 13 Judges (one from each member state plus one from France, Italy, Germany or the United Kingdom, by rotation) assisted by six Advocates-General (one from each of the five larger states plus one other, by rotation). Each Judge or Advocate-

Table A2.1   United Kingdom Members of the Economic and Social Committee for the period October 1986 to September 1990

Name	Affiliation
Mr Wilfred Aspinal	Executive Director, Managerial, Professional and Staff Liaison Group
Professor William Black	Former Professor of Economics, Queens University, Belfast
Mrs E Blatch	Leader, Cambridgeshire County Council
Mr Jack R Boddy	General Secretary, National Union of Agricultural and Allied Workers
Mr Ian M Campbell	Chairman, Scottish Railways Board
Mr Campbell Christie	General Secretary, Scottish Trades Union Congress
Mr John A de Normann	Director, Executive Committee of the National Council of Building Material Producers
Miss Ella G Dodds	Board Member, Northern Engineering Industries Parsons Ltd
Mr Kenneth J Gardner	Chairman, Mars European Food Legislation Committee
Mr Eric A B Hammond	General Secretary, Electrical, Electronic, Telecommunications and Planning Union
Mr Colin A Hancock	Company Director, Adviser to Enterprise and Deregulation Unit of the Department of Employment
Mr Tom Jenkins	Assistant Secretary, Trades Union Congress International Department
Miss Ada Maddocks	National Organizing Officer, National Association of Local Government Officers
Mr R J Moreland	Company Director and Management Consultant
Mr William G Poeton	President, Union of Independent Companies
Dr Anne Robinson	Senior Lecturer in Politics, University College, Cardiff
Mr Alex R Smith	General Secretary, National Union of Tailors and Garment Workers
Mr Larry J Smith	Executive Officer, Transport and General Workers' Union
Mr G H Speirs	Secretary, Convention of Scottish Local Authorities
Dr P Storie-Pugh	Former President, Royal College of Veterinary Surgeons
Mr M P Strauss	Coordinating Director (Policy), National Farmers Union
Mr Keith M Tamlin	Secretary, Mail Order Traders' Association
Mr F.J Whitworth	Deputy Director General, General Council of British Shipping
Mrs A Williams	President, National Federation of Consumer Groups

Source: Reference 5

General is required to be independent and to possess the qualifications required for the highest judicial positions in their respective countries.

The Judges and Advocates-General are appointed to exert judicial control over the institutions of the Community and Member States. The Advocates-General review the evidence on cases brought before the Court and present reasoned and independent submissions to the Court which generally sits in plenary session with all Judges present.

References

1. *Treaty Establishing the European Economic Community* signed in Rome 25 March 1957. An abridged version of this treaty is published in *Treaties Establishing the European Communities*. Office for Official Publications of the European Communities, Luxembourg. 1983
2. *European Communities Act, 1972*. Eliz 2 (1972 ch 8). HMSO, London. 1972
3. *Single European Act* signed at Luxembourg on 17 February 1986 and at The Hague on 28 February 1986. Published in Council of the European Communities *Single European Act and Final Act*. Office for Official Publications of the European Communities, Luxembourg. 1986
4. *European Communities (Amendment) Act, 1986* Eliz 2 (1986 ch 58). HMSO, London. 1986
5. A full list of the members of the Economic and Social Committee is given in *Bulletin of the Economic and Social Committee* No 8–9. 1986. Office for Official Publications of the European Communities, Luxembourg. 1986

Appendix 3   Key addresses

Donald Thompson, MP
Ministry of Agriculture, Fisheries and Food
Whitehall Place
London SW1A 2HH
  Minister with responsibility for food

Anthony Newton, MP
Department of Health and Social Security
Alexander Fleming House
Elephant and Castle
London SE1 6BY
  Minister responsible for health including health aspects of foods

Your Member of Parliament
House of Commons
Westminster
London SW1A OAA
  May be willing to support any initiatives for change by asking questions or lobbying Ministers and Parliamentary colleagues. Even if un-
willing to act in the House every MP will respond to clear, specific
questions. Usually your MP will get the appropriate Minister or department to provide a reply.

Standards Division
Ministry of Agriculture, Fisheries and Food
Great Westminster House
Horseferry Road
London SW1P 2AE
  Government department responsible for drawing up most new food
regulations

The Scottish Home and Health Department
St Andrew's House
Edinburgh EH1 3HE
  Responsible for food legislation in Scotland

Department of Health and Social Services
Food Control Branch
Room 6 Annex A Donaldson House
Upper Newtonards Road
Belfast BT4 3SF
Responsible for food legislation in Northern Ireland

Commission of the European Communities (London Office)
8 Storey's Gate
London SW1P 3AT
Contact for list of European Documentation Centre Addresses
Contact regarding European legislation

Commission of the European Communities
200 rue de la Loi
1049 Brussels
Belgium
Contact for list of European Documentation Centre Addresses
Contact regarding European legislation

Office of the United Kingdom Permanent Representative to the
European Community
Rond Point Robert Schuman 6
1040 Brussels
Belgium
The United Kingdom's permanent representative to the European
Community acts to co-ordinate the views of various UK interests in
EEC decision making

Joint FAO/WHO Food Standards Programme
FAO
00100 - Rome
Italy
For further information regarding the activities of the Codex
Alimentarius Commission and its subsidiary bodies

Food and Drink Federation
6 Catherine Street
London WC2 5JJ
Principal trade association for the British food manufacturing
industry

Federation des Industries Agricoles et Alimentaires
Avenue de Cortenbergh 172 bte 7
B 1040 Brussels
Belgium
Principal association representing the interests of the European food
and agriculture industries to the institutions of the European
Communities

Retail Consortium
1–19 New Oxford Street
London WC1A 1PA
  Principal trade association representing British retailing interests

Consumers' Association
14 Buckingham Street
London WC2N 6DS
  A membership organization with 800 000 subscribers. Campaigning is
research-led and includes pressure on Government and business.
Publishes *Which?* magazine

Consumers in the European Community Group
24 Tufton Street
London SW1P 3RB
  The umbrella body for 27 voluntary and professional groups with an
interest in the impact of EEC legislation on UK consumer affairs

National Consumer Council
20 Grosvenor Gardens
London SW1W ODH
  Set up by government around ten years ago. Its job is to identify the
interests of consumers and to represent those interests to central and
local government, the nationalized industries and private industry and
business, and the public and professional services. The Council is
funded by the Department of Trade and Industry

Bureau European des Unions de Consommateurs
Rue Royale 29, bte 3
B - 1000 Brussels
Belgium
  A consortium of consumer organizations in the Member States of the
European Community

FACT
Room W
25 Horsell Road
London N5 1XL
  Organization currently campaigning for changes to legislation relating
to the use of food additives

Local Authorities Coordinating Body on Trading Standards
PO Box 6
Fell Road
Croydon CR9 1LP
  Coordinates the activities of trading standards officers employed by
local authorities

Trading Standards Department
Your County Council or Metropolitan District Council
  The local authority department which enforces food laws and which
can influence or contribute to the deliberations of many of the above.

Institute of Trading Standards Administration
Metropolitan House
37 Victoria Avenue
Southend-on-Sea SS2 6DA
   Professional association for trading standards officers

Association of Public Analysts
30 Russell Square
London WC1B 5DT
   Professional association for public analysts

Institution of Environmental Health Officers
Chadwick House
48 Rushworth Street
London SE1 0QT
   Professional association for environmental health officers

Index